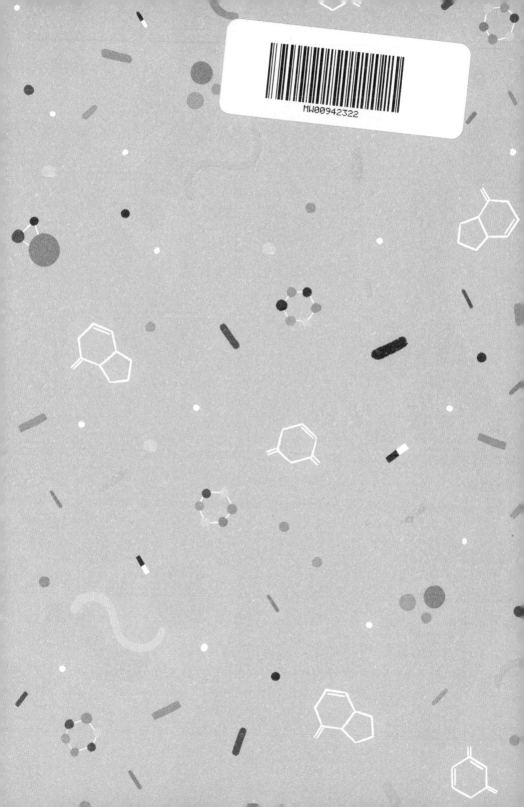

MW00942322

WHAT MAKES US HUMAN

Professor Luke O'Neill is a world-renowned immunologist and a professor of biochemistry at Trinity College Dublin. He is the author of four bestselling books, including *The Great Irish Science Book* for children. Luke is a member of the Royal Irish Academy and is a fellow of the Royal Society.

Tara O'Brien is an illustrator from Dublin, Ireland. Her work has a focus on diverse representations of people, body politics, mental health and our connection to nature.

WHAT MAKES
US HUMAN

A SCIENTIST'S GUIDE TO OUR
AMAZING EXISTENCE

PROFESSOR LUKE O'NEILL

GILL BOOKS

Gill Books
Hume Avenue
Park West
Dublin 12
www.gillbooks.ie

Gill Books is an imprint of M.H. Gill and Co.

9780717193769

Adapted from *Humanology* by James Doyle
Illustrations by Tara O'Brien
Designed by Graham Thew
Edited by Sheila Armstrong
Proofread by Tess Tattersall
Printed and bound by Printer Trento, Italy
This book is typeset in Quasimoda.

The paper used in this book comes from the wood pulp
of sustainably managed forests.

A CIP catalogue record for this book is available from the British Library.

5 4 3 2 1

MIX
Paper | Supporting
responsible forestry
FSC® C015829
FSC
www.fsc.org

ACKNOWLEDGEMENTS

A big thanks to James Doyle for turning
Humanology into *What Makes Us Human*,
Tara O'Brien for her wonderful illustrations,
and Sheila Armstrong for excellent editing.

CONTENTS

INTRODUCTION

Welcome to *What Makes Us Human*!

This book is all about what it is that makes you human. It might seem obvious. I mean, you haven't got four legs and a tail! (Unless you're a very smart dog reading this, and if you are, you're welcome too!) But what you *have* got is lots of interesting things going on which make you a fascination.

If an alien came to Earth (how many movies have you seen about that – they're always great, right?), had a good look at you, and compared you with other life forms on Earth, the alien would spot that you're very interesting indeed. You walk upright, wear clothes, cook your food, laugh and make jokes, play music, build machines, and think about the deep questions like 'How did we get here?'

It's those deep questions that this book will try to answer. But we'll need some help to figure it out … enter science. Science is based on carefully observing some aspects of the world, asking questions, coming up with ideas and then doing experiments to see if the ideas are correct.

So, let's say there's a new disease – dare I mention COVID-19? Scientists observed the effects of the disease, asked questions and did experiments, which led to the discovery of the virus that causes COVID-19. Then, more questions and experiments lead to the development of the tremendous vaccines that are protecting us, and also the therapies that we can use against COVID-19.

All of this only happened because of all the things that make us human – our curiosity, our brains and our special abilities. But where did those most excellent abilities come from? In this book, I will take you on a journey to find out.

We'll begin with the very origin of life itself, which scientists currently think started a very long time ago – around 4 billion years! – when the first cell appeared on Earth. That cell then evolved and evolved until, finally, it got to our species, *Homo sapiens sapiens*, which means 'clever clever human'. (I'll tell you one thing, you're very clever. But because I'm a scientist I need evidence to prove that, and the evidence is that you're reading my book. Now, to prove you really are clever, keep reading to find out what scientists think about how you got so brainy.)

I'll tell you all about the science of love (it's all about chemicals … or is it?) and how a sperm fertilises an egg, which then develops into a human being using something remarkable called DNA. Then we'll look at how children develop and learn, and see how the messers at the back of the class might be on the right track. We'll talk God, too, and why you should never go into the deep, dark forest.

Your sense of humour and love of music make you truly unique among species, so we'll look at the science behind those things too. And then I will tell you all about your body clock and the rhythm of your life, why you feel sleepy or hungry. You'll also find out what we think sleep is actually for!

Next, I will tell you about important medical topics and the search for new medicines (and whether we can ever make a superhero – even that isn't too far-fetched, as we learn to control DNA!). And, of course, I will tell you about how robots will take over the world (or will they?) and how the future will have driverless cars. Then we'll look at two massive machines that are changing the way we think about the universe.

Next, I will tell you what happens when you get older, what happens to your body after you die (the gory part – get ready for maggots). You'll learn how you might be able to have your body frozen and be brought back to life!

On a happier note, I will tell you how we might become extinct as a species, although that will most likely happen long after you've gone. But did you know that life almost became extinct on six separate occasions, but somehow managed to survive? If it hadn't, you wouldn't be reading this, because I wouldn't exist to have written it for you to read, if you know what I mean. Cheery, eh?

But don't despair, because I will finish with how, right now, things have never been better for us humans. All the signs show that things will continue to improve for our species, and hopefully all life on Earth. You have an awful lot to look forward to, not least the enjoyment I hope you will get from reading this book.

I can tell you all these things because of what science has told us. Science is great and hugely satisfying. It's hard work, and it's taken us a long, long, long time to figure out what we now know. There have been some strange detours along the way – we'll talk about leeches, chicken's bumholes, weeing on seeds and a universe full of paperclips. But it's (mostly!) been an upward journey.

If you're scientifically minded, you must follow the motto of the world's oldest scientific society, the Royal Society in London, founded by Isaac Newton, Robert Boyle and other scientists in 1660. Their motto is *'nullius in verba,'* or 'take nobody's word for it'. In other words: show me the evidence! We need to always ask questions about the world around us. At scientific gatherings, you're only truly listened to if you have the data to back up what you're saying.

Science is a great comfort to us in this crazy, confusing and sometimes upsetting world. It has always been a great friend to me, and I hope it will be a friend to you too, and that this book will help you feel that way. So come on, join me now. Get stuck in. And remember: always be questioning, always be wondering and always have fun. Hey, you're a scientist already!

CHAPTER 1

WELCOME, O LIFE! HOW LIFE GOT STARTED

SOME PEOPLE THINK that life began with two hippies and a talking snake. Others believe in a giant cosmic egg or a rainbow serpent that shook the world into life. Some of these might be true, and certainly many millions of people still believe in some of these creation myths. But remember – as scientists, we need to take nobody's word for it and do our own investigations.

So, what does the evidence tell us about that very important question: How did life begin on Earth? To try to answer this, we need to use everything that science has to throw at a problem – from chemistry to biology to geology and even astrophysics. It's a great puzzle, and science at its best is about solving puzzles. Still, scientists still have no *full* answer to the question of how rocks and minerals somehow formed a living thing. How could a lump of clay become alive? But there has been great progress, and we now have a reasonable understanding of how life began, and of how that life led to us humans.

AGEING THE EARTH

But to figure that out, we first needed to understand what Planet Earth itself is. Otherwise, it would be putting the cart before the horse, and the poor horse would be very confused. So, how old is the Earth? Think back to something you did a year ago. We can grasp 10 years passing; it might be that long since you were born. But how about 1,000 years? A hundred thousand years? A million years? Such time spans are well beyond our understanding.

So, it's understandable that, for many years, people thought the Earth was much younger than it actually is. An Irish Bishop, James Ussher, gets the credit for the first attempt to figure out exactly how old our planet is. He went to the library to work it out, using mainly the Bible for evidence. (A library is a place where old people went to borrow books. Why bother when you can go online?) His best guess was very specific – the Earth was created on 22 October 4004 BC. And he went even further, claiming that creation began at 6 p.m. and was finished by midnight that night ... just six hours? That's fast work – just 12 episodes of your favourite TV show.

Then, in 1899, another Irishman, a physicist this time, took another stab at it. John Joly based his guess on how salty the oceans are (there was no mention of vinegar) and came up with about 90 million years as the age of the Earth. Better, but not quite there yet!

Finally, scientists managed to get it right with a method called radiometry, which measures the amount of radioactivity in rocks. Using this, they could figure out the age of the Earth, which is ... drum roll please ... 4.54 billion years old!

We now know that when the solar system settled into its current layout, Earth formed when gravity (a universal force which pulls all matter together) pulled swirling gas and dust in to become the third planet from the sun. This took a lot longer than six hours – sorry Mr Ussher! In fairness, lots of really smart people got things wrong along the way, but that's the beauty of science and learning. We can all make mistakes. That's part of working out the evidence and taking nobody's word for it.

ONE SUPER CELL

Those rocks tell us more than just the age of the Earth – they also tell us that the atmosphere on the young Earth was full of toxic chemicals. This wasn't a very hospitable place for life to set up camp, so there was nobody home for millions of years.

Instead, there was a vast, bubbling cauldron with random chemicals forming and being destroyed and reacting with one another. There was also heat from vents in the sea floor and lots of lightning strikes, which gave the chemicals energy to hit off each other and react. It's as if the Earth was a giant test tube full of chemicals and gases, with electricity sparking inside and a fire underneath it. And, somehow, all these random chemical reactions gave us the first living creature! There should have been some great blast of trumpets, or even a round of applause. But, sadly, there was no one about to notice.

Scientists know that this happened around 4.28 billion years ago. But this first creature wasn't anything nearly as complex as you or me, or even your hamster. It was a single-celled creature we call a bacterium. It sucked up loads of nutrients (like your teacher slurping coffee), divided and made baby bacteria. Scientists even gave it a name – LUCA. This stands for Last Universal Common Ancestor, and no, it wasn't Italian! LUCA is like the great-great-great-great (insert a lot more greats here) grandparent of all life on Earth.

It's hard to get your head around the idea that all life came from this one single cell (a bit like algebra), but we now know that humans make up just 0.01 per cent of all living things on Earth. Most of what is around us is found in plants and bacteria, and while we are truly brilliant creatures, we shouldn't get big heads. Why? The tiny 0.01 per cent that is humanity has managed to destroy 83 per cent of Planet Earth's wild animals and almost half of all plants ... oops.

The big problem we face in trying to explain how this first spark of life came about is very difficult because the chemicals involved are very fragile. They don't like heat (look what happens when you boil an egg – it changes completely) or acid, or even oxygen. The last one always shocks people, as we often see oxygen as essential for life. It is for humans as we need it to ... like, breathe? But oxygen is also very toxic. Well, to understand how life managed to defy the odds, we need to go back to a fairy tale.

If you haven't read Goldilocks and the Three Bears, then all you need to know is that one day a sweet little girl with beautiful golden locks (old-speak for hair) was wandering about the forest. She decided to break into the three bears' house – rude! – when they were out doing whatever bears do on a workday. She proceeded to sit in their chairs, watch Netflix, eat their porridge, then sleep in their beds ... what a chancer! But some of the stuff she tried out didn't suit. For example, the first porridge she tried was too hot, the second too cold, but the third was just right. The same with the beds – one was too big, the other too small, but the third was just right.

So, back on the young Planet Earth, it took a long time for things to become 'just right'. But the stars eventually aligned, and the first cell that would lead directly to us appeared. Up popped LUCA, ready to eat all the porridge. And LUCA was able to copy itself, but – and this is important – each time it did, it made a few mistakes. This meant that some cells were slightly different, which resulted in different species. Some of these cells were better able to survive to copy themselves. This is what's known as survival of the fittest – evolution.

In a very short period, 541 million years ago, most types of animals appeared on Earth in a 20–25 million year 'window' (I know, that's a big window, but in the history of everything, this was pretty quick) called the Cambrian Explosion.

It's been a long, long, *long* journey from LUCA to us. Humans are a recent arrival to Earth. The best way to imagine the length of time we humans have been on this rock is to look at the whole history of the Earth like it is one single day made up of 24 hours. If you do that, you will see that we arrived at the party, all excited with presents and looking for cake, at 17 seconds to midnight. Urgh! Story of my life. Missed all the fun!

PLANT POWER

A big moment came some 3 billion years ago, when plants arrived. We often think plants just stand there being green, but they are the key to all life on Earth. They are the only things on Earth that can harness the sun's energy to make food, which we eventually eat. This process is called photosynthesis.

There are no species other than plants that can do this amazing trick. You see, plants like boring grass and annoying hedges look like they are completely pointless, but without them, we would all be done for. Let me explain. Imagine you carried out your very own science experiment: it's a lovely sunny day and you place three things outside in the sun for, say, five hours.

Thing A is a long roll of grass. Thing B is a cow (I know, where does anyone find a cow at short notice? But stick with me on this). Thing C is an annoying cousin or classmate. You place them all in the sun for five hours. Thing B will not change in any way, except get a bit hot and need a lie-down under a tree afterwards. Thing C will possibly faint, certainly turn red, blotchy and get sunburnt, but nothing else. Thing A, however, will have made itself all the food it needs for that day. Yes, plants are the driving force for all life. No animal or human can use the sun to make their own food. It doesn't matter how long we are left in the sun, we can't do the plant magic trick. So, how did we get food

before Chinese takeaways opened? A by-product of photosynthesis is oxygen. As I said, oxygen is a toxic gas. It oxidises things, which is what happens when iron rusts. So life had to come up with a way to handle oxygen. And lo and behold it did. Through survival of the fittest, cells that could handle oxygen survived. And you know what? You are descended from that cell. Oxygen gave life a turbo boost!

It's amazingly simple and complex at the same time. You see, Things A, B and C worked together on this. The grass used the sun to make its own sugars or food. The cow moseyed over and thought, 'Mmm ... tasty grass,' and started to have a munch. The cow filled up on grass all day and was so stuffed it needed a good lie-down. Then a human arrived with a shiny new spear and the poor moo-cow ended up as the first McWhopper. The human enjoyed their meal, burped and had a nice sleep after a very, very hard day at the woolly mammoth shop. Thanks, plants!

LIFE OUT THERE

On a freakier note, scientists are discovering more and more planets where the conditions are just right for life – this is called the Goldilocks zone. At the last count, we have counted 40 billion of these planets, which are just the right distance from their stars to allow the chemistry for life to kick off, just like on Planet Earth. Scientifically and mathematically, that means we are unlikely to be alone. ET might be out there somewhere, eating crisps and binge-watching *The Simpsons* or *Countdown* ...

One recent candidate to support life is the moon called Enceladus – not to be confused with enchiladas, which are nicer to eat than a dusty rock. Enceladus spends its days orbiting Saturn. In a 1997 NASA/European Space Agency mission, the probe Cassini was sent there. This spaceship left Earth and travelled a mind-blowing 1.272 billion miles, arriving at Enceladus some seven years later on 1 July 2004. This was an incredible journey. If you drove a car the same distance at 50km per hour, it would take you 3,000 years to get there! (That's with no pee breaks either.)

But why did we go there at all? Well, scientists had observed huge jets of steam breaking through the thick ice that covers Enceladus, and they wanted to know what they were made of. Cassini went in and found out that the steam was made of free hydrogen – a brilliant source of energy. This is the kind of energy plants make from photosynthesis using sunlight. It is the energy that kickstarts life. What we don't know is whether one of these perfect planets will hold intelligent life like us ... Yes, I meant you! Scientists are confident that these planets will house other living systems, but whether they evolve into complex beings is the big question. Even bigger than if they've invented porridge yet.

CHAPTER 2

HOW
WE GOT
TO BE
SO
SMART

EVEN THOUGH THE body you are currently driving around in is almost identical to the 200,000-year-old model your ancient ancestor used, us *Homo sapiens* have made mega-strides in a relatively short time. We're all descended from people who lived 200,000 years ago. Our full title is *Homo sapiens sapiens*, which actually means 'wise, wise human' – that means we must be very wise, but that wasn't always the case. It's not that long ago that we rubbed our poo on the end of arrows to shoot at and poison our enemies. Or rubbed a chicken's bumhole on our armpits in the hope it would cure the Black Death ... Yeah, that was us!

Anyway, you have to feel sorry for the people back then. After all, imagine a world with no smartphones, no space stations and no clue about things like viruses or that Interweb thing ... What's a WiFi? But that's why we are so brilliant. We could take a person from back then and educate them to the level we are at now. We could turn them into airline pilots or doctors or politicians. All that's happened is that in 200,000 years we figured out a lot of things.

Originally, we would have used our unique intelligence to help us simply survive. We could predict if a drought was coming, protect our children, work as a team to kill dinner (there was no Deliveroo, sorry!), and work out how to deal with losing a loved one. What is important is why we are so different from any other species on Earth. The key scientific question is: How did we become us?

THE PERFECT RECIPE

As ever with this kind of question, we must start with DNA. DNA – or deoxyribonucleic acid, to give its full name – is the recipe to make all living things. This recipe is written in a chemical code that is made up of building blocks called nucleotides. These are like very tiny beads on a string, each nucleotide being a different bead. There are only four nucleotides, which go by their letter: A, T, C and G. These are strung together to make up your chromosomes – the structures that contain DNA.

Incredibly, the total number of beads strung out along the chromosomes in you is 6 billion. That's an awful lot of beads, and an awful lot of threading, and yet it's real. But it's even more wonderful, because DNA is actually made of two separate strings that wrap around each other, twisting into the iconic double helix shape. This arrangement makes it stable, a bit like a ladder, though twisted around its centre.

When James Watson, Francis Crick, Maurice Wilkins and Rosalind Franklin, the scientists who first discovered that shape, realised what it was they couldn't believe it. They ran to their local pub (The Eagle in Cambridge) and exclaimed, 'We've found the secret of life!' Why did they say that? Well, if we look at the two strings that wrap around one another, we see something quite remarkable. We see that if there is an A bead on one string, it always pairs with a T bead on the other. They click together a bit like LEGO blocks. If there is a C bead on one string, there is always a G bead on the other string. These are a bit like the rungs on the ladder that connect the two sides.

This suggested to Watson and Crick that the way we pass on information to make a new cell involves the two strings unravelling from each other. Then, a new string is made one bead at a time, each bead clicking into place by bonding with its corresponding bead on the single string. In a moment, they had found the secret of life – how information is passed on to the next generation. The rule of A clicking into T and C clicking into G applies in all forms of life on Earth, and initially arose in the first cell, from which all other cells are descended (our friend LUCA again).

Now, once you have the sequence of the beads on the string – the DNA that tells us the order of the A, T, C and G – you have the recipe for life. But very importantly the sequence instructs the cell to make proteins in a very complex process. Runs of nucleotides called genes make specific proteins – the building blocks of life. The proteins then make you the living creature that you are – they might give you horns on your head or determine whether you're hairy or tall or short.

We can compare different species with each other in terms of their DNA sequence. An Irish molecular biologist called Des Higgins and his colleagues came up with a computer program to do just that: to align DNA sequences and compare how similar they are. (Bet they were still playing Minecraft in the background, though.)

It turns out that half of the beads on the string from a banana are in roughly the same sequence as half of the beads on the string from a human. We share half our recipe with bananas. Sadly, some of my friends are probably slightly more banana than human.

When we compare ourselves with chimpanzees and bonobos, our recipes are around 95 per cent identical, confirming our close shared ancestry. We had a common ancestor some 2 million years ago, a creature that looked a lot like a chimpanzee. It had offspring and one of those became our ancestor and another became the ancestor of chimps or bonobos. Gradually over time, a 5 per cent difference in the DNA sequence became apparent. Remember, as we saw in the last chapter, every time the DNA recipe is copied, a tiny mistake is made. These mistakes are why we are 5 per cent different to chimpanzees. The trouble is, we don't know what is in that 5 per cent that makes us smartphone-using creatures and the chimp not. It might be a recipe to make our vocal cords better at speaking or wiring in the brain that allows us to think better. We just don't know.

One theory is that humans have a special trait called 'inventiveness'. We learned to make tools and fire. We learned that we needed clothes to counter the disadvantages of climate. Next, we learned that cooking food helped us digest it and extract more energy. We became stronger, faster and smarter. We started to walk upright, which gave us another advantage: it freed our hands up.

This made us more efficient hunters and better able to watch out for dangers around us.

Then we became social and started to place ourselves in a pecking order. We became status obsessed, a bit like that snobby auntie you hate talking to at Christmas who tells you that her perfume is made from the Himalayan wonder blossom that only flowers once every 10 years on a Tuesday at half ten. On a serious note, the obsession with status explains so much about us today and influences so many of our decisions from the house we live in, the car we drive, to the trainers we like.

Our natural desire to learn more and explore drove us to become the most successful and dominant species on Earth. Other animals have these traits too, but not to the extent of our brilliance. Chimpanzees can strip a twig of its leaves and use it as a tool to catch insects, and gorillas can use walking sticks to help them cross deep rivers, but the truth is that we are miles ahead. We can make art, music, poetry and perform plays. No other animal is as artistic as us, spending as much time as we do creating or appreciating art. And no other animal goes to the trouble that we do to look after our dead loved ones.

All of this happened on the savannahs of Africa. We take these traits with us as we move around the world. This begins around 90,000 years ago. We begin to get restless and we start to move out of Africa. The evidence of this is based on the dating of fossils from human bones. Maybe it happened because of overcrowding, or because of an accident – a tribe wandered over into the Middle East and couldn't get back. Evidence suggests that only a small number of our ancestors made this journey, and that all Europeans, Asians and Americans are descended from this intrepid group.

We move into a part of the world where plants are easy to grow. We notice this initially perhaps when we drop seeds from a plant and see that the same plant grows there. And so we discover farming. This meant we had to live in bigger communities and stay in the same place. This was a bad move, as we got sick from diseases that jumped between us, or perhaps hopped on us from our domesticated animals like pigs and goats.

Things then became unequal with the lucky few making up the 'haves' (the people who own the seeds or land) and the majority of people suffering as 'have-nots' (the people who have to work for them). We got greedy, started to travel and wanted to take over other tribes. The Europeans were especially good at taking over other places and we carved up the Americas and Africa. Unfortunately, we still live in a very unequal society today.

FAMILY MATTERS

The move out of Africa also leads to an encounter with a distant cousin: Neanderthals, in Europe some 70,000 years ago. They are another species of *Homo*, with whom we shared an ancestor about 600,000 years ago. Some of the descendants of that ancestor became us – the clever cousin who got all the points in his Leaving Cert (or whatever the equivalent might have been all those years ago).

The Neanderthals didn't do quite so well in terms of brain power (although recent work is challenging this), but they nonetheless thrived. At one point, scientists think there were as many as a million of them living in Europe. And then they encounter us, and within about 5,000 years they die out. We probably wipe them out because we outsmart them. Or maybe we gave them a nasty germ that they couldn't fight. Or we might simply have swamped them rather than slaughtered them, as our population grew.

Surprisingly, some of the genes we carry came from Neanderthals. We are all descended from the offspring of our matings with Neanderthals – the classic knuckle-dragging cavemen of movies, with their thick foreheads, and with limited evidence that they were in any way artistic like us or that they buried their dead. Evidence for these things may well still be uncovered, however, so we can't be certain. What we can be certain about is that humans and Neanderthals were very close neighbours indeed. We now know that around 1.8 per cent of our DNA came from Neanderthals. Some of my friends may have slightly more ...

One of the genes is a recipe for pale skin pigmentation. This means Europeans owe their pale skin partly to Neanderthals (we were dark-skinned when we came out of Africa). The pale skin is likely to have given us an advantage in the northern hemisphere, where the sun is weaker. Our skin makes Vitamin D in response to sunlight, which is important for the health of our bones, among other things, and the pale skin allows for maximum penetration of sunlight. So Neanderthal DNA might have helped us adapt to life outside Africa.

Not all of the Neanderthal DNA is beneficial, though. Some of it makes us more susceptible to certain diseases. Our lifestyle may have been different to the Neanderthals (for example, our diet), and this combined with these Neanderthal genes might put us at more of a risk of these diseases.

Finally, we also got from Neanderthals genes that boosted our immune systems. Neanderthals probably evolved these genes to survive the harsher conditions in Europe, where injury may have been more common (possibly because of violence between Neanderthals, although we don't know) and therefore infection more likely. Neanderthals with stronger immune systems survived, and passed those genes on to us.

If we move outside Europe to Asia, we find evidence that there was interbreeding with another *Homo* species, called Denisovans. These were closely related to Neanderthals (and us). Evidence suggests that Denisovans interbred with *Homo sapiens* too, and passed on genes, which can be seen in Melanesians (who live in Papua New Guinea) and indigenous Australians.

The latter deserve a special mention, as they reached Australia around 60,000 years ago, long before their cousins went into Europe. They are like the relation who goes travelling, leaving the family behind. Then, many thousands of years later, in 1770, the long-lost descendants of this branch of the family are finally reunited when Captain Cook lands in Australia. This family reunion, however, doesn't go so well for the Aborigine cousins, who should have hidden behind the sofa when the relatives came knocking on the door. They are still paying the price for this reunion.

Our current view of these three branches of Homo is that they are all descended from a species that lived between 300,000 and 400,000 years ago in Africa. One branch moves into the Middle East and then splits, with some of their descendants becoming Neanderthals, who move into Europe, and another branch becoming Denisovans, who move into Asia. By 130,000 years ago, those who stayed in Africa eventually evolve into us – Homo sapiens.

Some 75,000 years ago we ourselves move and go to Europe and Australasia, but we interbreed with our long-lost cousins, the Neanderthals in Europe, and the Denisovans in Asia. Around 20,000 years ago the Asian branch moves on to the Americas and their descendants are the Native Americans.

Finally, in 1492, there is another reunion – this time of the European branch of the family with their cousins who had travelled through Asia to the Americas. This is a family that had been separated for at least 40,000 years. Again, this doesn't end well for the Native Americans. The Americas, though, are perhaps the big melting pot, where all of the branches of Homo sapiens, be they those carrying

a bit of Neanderthal DNA or those carrying a bag of Denisovan DNA, can mix and mingle their DNA, bringing all kinds of advantages and challenges yet to be worked out.

Whatever way you look at it, despite the odd mistake, we are one big, clever family sharing this amazingly beautiful planet. So, like all the best families, we should stop fighting and try to get along with our brilliant brothers and sisters. After all, it took an awful lot of evolution, mistakes, adventures and exploration to get to the perfection that is you.

CHAPTER 3

THE

SCIENCE

OF

FINDING

LOVE

ITHOUT LOVE, NONE of us would be here. It's what made each and every one of us. We all started out as a sperm and an egg – yes, you were once an egg. Not a boiled one or a fried one, and not even a Cadbury's Crème one, but you were a little egg once. And then just nine months later you had grown into you: a perfect little egglet – I mean, human.

Today, if a woman thinks she is pregnant, she goes through a ritual of having to do a wee on a plastic stick that tells her if she definitely is or isn't. These practices have been going on for centuries. The ancient Egyptians had their own advice for a possibly pregnant 'mummy'. Ha! See what I did there? Sorry, anyway. The

Egyptians would ask the possibly pregnant woman to take a wee on some wheat seeds, and if the seeds started to sprout then it meant the woman was pregnant. Crazy or what? But what's crazier is that it worked, and scientists have proved that this test still works today.

But before all that, there's a long way to go.

AN ATTRACTIVE IDEA

Why do some people get together in the first place? Dating agencies have been around for a long time. In times past, the job of the matchmaker, who helped couples get together, was an important one. In ancient Rome, the god Cupid was thought to bring people together, as the process even then seemed mysterious. In the late twentieth century, someone invented speed-dating as a way to make the whole thing more efficient.

When it comes to instant physical attraction, we are often unable to explain why it happened. One problem is studying it in a scientific way. It's almost impossible to replicate attraction in a laboratory context. Those bright lights and people in white coats are clearly off-putting! So what do we know about that moment when you see someone across a crowded room and think, 'Hmmm, I like the look of them?'

First, there's the amazing world of what scientists call 'pheromones', or magic chemicals that come out of our sweat. I know, I've smelt your socks and even Harry Potter couldn't work his magic on those bad boys. But pheromones are well known to play a role in the animal kingdom, so why not in humans? Female dogs that are ready to mate will release pheromones and male dogs many miles away can detect them and start howling. Insects mainly attract a mate by releasing pheromones. This type of communication is subconscious – we don't even know that it's happening. It makes perfect sense (or scents).

A vast amount of money has been spent on researching pheromones. I can hear you say, 'What?! On researching sweat!' but it's true and very big business for perfume and aftershave makers, whose dream is to make the perfect love potion. But I'm not sure you'd want to be involved in some of these studies – they involve sniffing sweaty T-shirts! – and they still haven't figured out the magic ingredients.

Some recent surprising scientific findings might shed more light on the question of attraction. One of these findings is that we are inclined to choose people like ourselves. In fact, it has been shown that you are attracted to people who look like your own relatives. First response: Ew! Why this is the case isn't clear, but it could be down to a lower risk of being rejected. If you choose someone very different to you, they might see you as being from another tribe and might worry that you are going to harm them. Or, perhaps someone who looks like a relative is more likely to stick around and help you raise the baby. In one study, it was shown that we are attracted to people who look like our parents! Double ew.

Amazingly, the scientific research has pointed out some other strange things we fancy, like symmetry. Yes, symmetry is something your maths teacher is always banging on about, but with a quick Google search (or if you have an old-fashioned thing called 'a dictionary,') you will find out that the word 'symmetry' basically means one-half of something looks exactly like the other half. Scientists have worked out that we like symmetry in other people's faces. This symmetry apparently means we are healthy and have good genes and are a good choice to raise a child with.

The next weird thing scientists say we like are fingers. Yes, fingers, and not even fish fingers or the chocolate ones, but the real pointy, wrinkly ones on the end of your arms. In fact, buckle up for this one. Scientists say women look at a man's ring finger, not to check if he is

already taken by someone nor to see if he has dirty fingernails, but to assess the length. Now, wait for it … a long ring finger relative to the index finger means the dude was exposed to more of a hormone called testosterone in the womb. Apparently, the more testosterone a man was exposed to, the more healthy sperm he has and the more fertile he is. Beware, though, the scientists also say that men with long ring fingers are more likely to be unfaithful. I'm not pointing the finger at anybody, but you have been warned.

In truth, we all look for different things. Some women like tall men with broad shoulders and a big jaw, and some don't. Some studies say women also like men who do dangerous things, like sky diving or rally driving or being chased down the road by an angry bull. This, apparently, shows courage and bravery. I tend to think it points to stupidity, but what do I know. Confidence appears to be important to both men and women. Musicians and sportsmen and women are seen as confident and brave because they stand up in front of crowds and play despite the risk that something could go wrong. Part of their motivation is being admired/adored by others. However, overconfidence is to be avoided, so try not to get too big for your boots!

The good news is we are not just crude machines programmed to scan someone's body, smell them and then go for it. Personality (as every Rose of Tralee knows) counts too. Kindness has been shown to make someone more attractive. People were asked to rate the attractiveness of photographs of faces. Two weeks later they were asked to evaluate them again, but this time some were labelled as 'kind' or 'honest'. And guess what? Those labelled this way were more likely to be rated as attractive than they were the first time around.

What makes all these studies so difficult is that each of us seems to have individual preferences. Some prefer small feet, some prefer a business suit, some prefer bald men. There are some universal qualities that the majority of us rate highly, though: a clear complexion, shiny hair and cleanliness. These seem to be universal across all cultures, and are seen as signs of health, youth and good genes. But again, personality traits can dominate. There really does seem to be someone for everyone.

LOVE ON THE BRAIN

Once attraction kicks in, hormones in our brain step up and we effectively become addicted to the person. This is why we spend hours looking at their TikTok, or hang around in the rain to see them, or wait desperately for a message, or are compelled to go home via their street. Imaging studies of the brains of people in love have shown that the reward centre in the brain lights up like a beacon in people who are shown a photo of the one they are in love with.

But all of these responses eventually wear off, and the infatuation phase usually lasts from one to six months. It has to! Otherwise we would go nuts, and not do anything else all day other than gaze into the other person's eyes. Evolution had to make sure this would stop, as otherwise we would be eaten by a sabre-toothed tiger.

Afterwards, we become attached to the person, and that is driven by more hormones that give us the feeling of a warm hug. Why we stick around with that person is also to do with our brains – it's like we hear one particular song when we're in a great mood, then want to hear it again and again to produce the same feeling. So it's not so mysterious after all – it's just science. But understanding love doesn't make it any less special.

What might the future hold when it comes to our relationships? Well, perhaps one day lots of traits and genetic markers will be put into an algorithm and the program will find your perfect partner. There will be a more elaborate form of online matchmaking. And you will be helped in your goal if you spray yourself with Love Potion No. 9.

But surely it's more fun to find a mate in the wild, though?

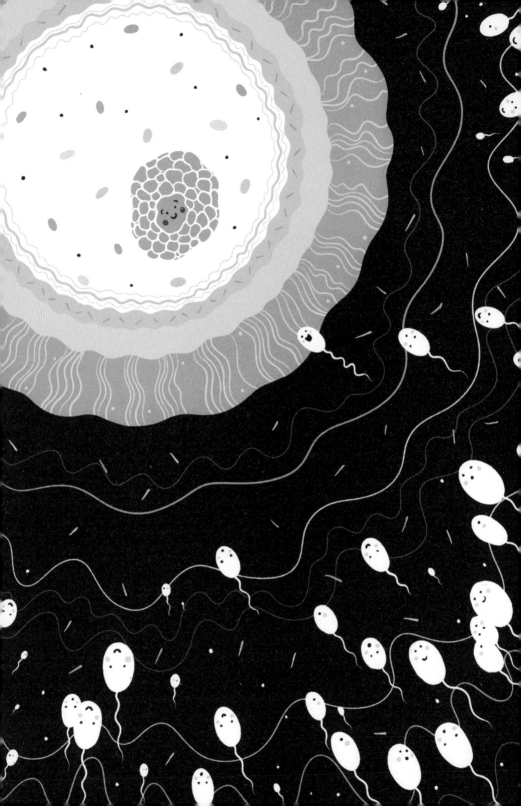

CHAPTER 4

SPERM MEETS EGG: THE SCIENCE OF FERTILITY

AS WE SAW in the last chapter, the science of attraction is about different signs and signals being sensed and transmitted in an attempt to draw us together. The purpose of this is simple: to get us to have sex and then look after the baby once it's born. It's clearly a highly complex process, and without it our species would die out. All those worries and ruses to achieve one thing: to get the DNA from one tiny microscopic sperm to fuse with the DNA inside a tiny microscopic egg – the moment of fertilisation. And yet we're here to tell the tale that this process has worked for us as a species for at least 200,000 years.

PANDA PROBLEMS

Some animals don't have it so easy. Take the panda bear. As adults, these lovable black-and-white creatures live on their own and rarely meet another panda. Even then, studies have shown they mightn't even bother to mate. And females only become ready to mate once a year in the spring for 12–25 days. But she's only actually fertile for up to 24 hours in that period – 24 hours in a whole year. So even if a lumbering, cute male panda meets a female, he might miss that 24-hour period. Who invented that? How have they survived as a species?

This is one reason why only around 1,600 pandas are left in the wild, so you probably won't see one in the Tesco carpark. It also presents a problem in trying to breed them in captivity, like in zoos. Even if the zookeeper creates the perfect ambience – they do their best to recreate the natural habitat for pandas, the equivalent of a romantic dinner for two – the pandas still might not mate. Zookeepers have noticed they don't seem to have a clue how to do it. And even if they do mate, how likely is it that the sperm will make it to the egg and fertilise it? The chances are low, and likely much lower than us humans, who in our prime can expect fertilisation to happen one in every four times.

Pandas' main method for plural panda production now is artificial insemination. This is where the egg is fertilised in a lab and put back into the female panda. This is one reason why they aren't a dominant species in the world today. Well, that and the fact that they don't have thumbs and sit around eating bamboo all day ...

LOCK AND KEY

So, back to humans: fertilisation. This is the moment, the purpose of all the choosing what clothes to wear, staying late at a party where the music is too loud, the endless text-messaging, second-guessing, hassle and joy of the mating game – the moment when a sperm finally gets to the egg.

Closer inspection will show that the hard work doesn't stop there, and making a new you has been a massive struggle. The odds of a single sperm fusing with an egg and making you are tiny. A single sperm has a 1 in 300 million chance of making it. It has to be the first, it has to outswim all the other sperm and it has to swim

a distance from Los Angeles to Hawaii. To give you an idea, that's almost 4,000km. That swim would give you sore arms all right, but even after that there are more obstacles. Only one in five sperm will swim in the right direction in the first place. And sometimes the woman's body will reject the sperm. Even if they get to the right spot, there is a tough skin around the egg that the sperm has to penetrate to deliver its precious cargo of DNA.

If it makes it past all these hurdles, now we get to the magic moment: when the sperm fuses with the egg. Despite the fact that this is critical for the whole process (and for the survival of our species), how it works has only recently been figured out. In 2005, a Japanese scientist called Okabe was studying the proteins that stud the surface of a sperm. He discovered that the proteins were brilliant at recognising other proteins. He found a protein that can unlock the egg, which he called 'Izumo' – named after the Japanese shrine to marriage. Sperm that didn't have Izumo might have got to the egg, high-fiving themselves for making it, but they couldn't break through the egg's hard protective shell. They didn't have a key to unlock the egg's door ... which must have been very annoying after swimming all that distance, and where do you go after that? Do you just get the bus home and huff all the way?

On the other side of the world, another scientist, Gavin Wright in the UK, found the lock part on the egg that matched up to Izumo's key. This was a special protein only found on the surface of unfertilised eggs. He named this egg protein Juno after the Roman goddess of fertility and marriage. Juno is very clever and unique. It only appears on the surface of unfertilised eggs. Once a sperm unlocks an egg, Juno starts to disappear from the egg's surface ... that's one clever egg.

Once the lock has been opened, the sperm dies as it squirts its DNA into the egg, joining the DNA from the mother. What is interesting here is that sperm and eggs are unique among all the cells in our body. Every other cell has the DNA arranged in 23 pairs of chromosomes. For sperm and egg cells, only a single set of 23 chromosomes occurs. When the 23 chromosomes from the egg fuse with the 23 chromosomes of the sperm, we're back to 23 pairs, a total of 46. Every cell will have the full set of DNA, since it gets copied in full every time a cell divides, starting with the fertilised egg. Each species of plants and animals has a set number of chromosomes. A fruit fly, for example, has 4 pairs of chromosomes, while a rice plant has 12 and a dog has 39.

The now fertilised egg, at first a single cell, divides, and then the two cells that result divide, and so on and so on, until they get to a fully developed foetus. What's interesting about this is the fact that the cells all start off the same – these are known as stem cells. Then they begin to specialise, becoming one of the many different kinds of cell in your body. Some become cells in your brain, some become cells in your skin. Some become cells in your liver, some become cells in your blood. Finally, all the cell types that make you are in place.

Sounds complex? Well, humans have been doing all this without instructions for hundreds of thousands of years ... Although maybe the poor pandas could do with having a look at a manual – at least it would be right there in black and white (sorry, no more panda jokes).

THE GENDER GAP

The shiny, new fertilised egg will either be male or female and this is dictated by the sperm. The rules are pretty simple: male means there is a special chromosome called the 'Y' chromosome. Female means the chromosome called the 'X' chromosome is present. The combinations will decide if we are born as boys or girls. An egg fertilised by a Y sperm cell will form a male, while an egg fertilised by an X sperm will be female.

For largely unknown reasons, there are always slightly more boys than girls born – 51 per cent to 49 per cent. Worryingly, we are seeing in some parts of the world that boys are on the decline. Could men become a thing of the past? An extinct species up there with the dodo and the woolly mammoth? No more males could mean no more humans. Oh dear!

In the developed world in the last 50 years, male sperm has halved, and fewer males are being born. What is the cause? Some scientists believe it might be due to climate change, pollution, obesity, smoking or plastics. In Canada, scientists found that in communities that were exposed to pollution from factories, the ratio shifts towards more females than males. Another study has found that male foetuses are especially sensitive to the effects of climate change. This means that one (more!) unimagined consequence of global warming may be that more females than males will be born.

Or maybe the loss of the male species is due to simpler things. Like watching too much TV. And no, your mum didn't pay me to write that. Studies show that men who watched 20 hours or more

TV a week had fewer sperm than men who watched just 15 hours or did more exercise.

The science shows that temperature plays an important role in this dilemma, as sperm like cool conditions. They aren't a fan of too much heat ... it doesn't suit them. Doctors will advise a prospective father that his best chances of making a brand-new human just like him will increase if he does the following (this is not a joke):

1. Wears loose underwear – yes, no more tighty-whities,
2. Stops slobbing around on the sofa all day, and
3. Doesn't ride a bike too much ... the seat appears to cause a problem ... ouch.

A real possibility is that humans may be made artificially in the future. It may one day be possible to take a skin cell, reprogramme it all the way back to a sperm cell, and then use that to fertilise an egg. Crazy as it may sound, scientists have managed to do just that using stem cells in mice. The stem cells have the capacity to be turned into any cell type, provided they are coaxed in the right direction. Mouse eggs were used in the study and, importantly, healthy baby mice were born.

It might even be possible to do the same in humans. Imagine it: taking skin to a lab and extracting the cells. Rewinding them to sperm level. Mixing with an egg in a dish. Letting Izumo meet Juno and hey presto! Just like *The Great British Bake Off*, you've made and baked a brilliant new human being to send off into the wild blue yonder.

CHAPTER 5

IRISH
MAMMIES
GOT
IT
RIGHT

WHAT IS THE scariest thing you can think of? You'll probably say a fierce sabre-toothed tiger, or a thing with three heads, or an alien that shoots lasers out of its eyeballs. But if you really thought about it, I mean, really got your brain in gear, you'd soon work out that the scariest thing you've ever encountered is a thing called 'Angry Mum'.

Think about it: you are at a relative's house, the supermarket or getting collected from school. You've done something wrong – and you know it. Mum meets another parent or relative and she's all nice and smiley. She nods her head and chats to the other mum/relative but then you have to leave and get in the car … Help! Please help! The car door shuts, and all hell is unleashed. Her voice goes up several octaves and you just wish that you were being attacked by a sabre-toothed tiger!

The truth is, Angry Mums will fight to the death for you. Hollywood and comic book bad guys are wimps in comparison. Mums know nothing is more important than you, and nothing will get in their way. They worry. They have worried about you since you were an egg. And they aren't the only ones. Your teachers worry about you. Even the politicians worry about you. You may not know it, but you've got a gang behind you and they're really rooting for you. Even when they're screaming at you like a banshee!

NATURE OR NURTURE?

In all seriousness, scientists, teachers and mammies have long debated where you will go and what influences that journey. One big theory is the idea of 'nature versus nurture'. Are your chances of success written in your genes? Or is your environment more important? The likely truth is that it's a combination of both nature and nurture – or, to be more precise, nature *through* nurture. You will reveal someone's genetic make-up by nurturing that person in a particular environment.

Say you have a child who has the genes to be a great drummer. If you give that child a drumkit, lots of books about drumming and a good music teacher, their skill will be revealed. (For their parents' sake, better give them a soundproofed room too.) But we have yet to figure out the genetic basis for being a good drummer – maybe we should take DNA samples from famous drummers to find out.

Another good comparison is cars. Let's say we are all cars with different engines – some more efficient than others. All cars need petrol. Some cars will run better than others (the nature of the engine), and on less petrol (the nurture to make them run). Again, it is nature *through* nurture – the nature of the engine will reveal itself based on how you nurture it with petrol. The environment is therefore critical for different cars. This might mean petrol, or the state of the roads. If the roads are bad, the car won't go anywhere, no matter how souped-up the engine. The genes people have are the things that make the brain (the parts list for the engine). But the environment is also needed to get the car to perform. This means that we need to always think about the environment a child is brought up in, both at home and at school, since there will be plenty of things that can be done to try to ensure that they have a chance. We need to fill in those potholes along the way.

The problem is that it's not easy to study how all this works – it takes a long time to see how a child develops, and there are always lots of what are called confounding variables. Say you collect data on sunburns and ice cream consumption. You find that higher ice cream consumption is associated with a higher probability of sunburn. Does that mean ice cream consumption causes sunburn? Study design is everything in psychology. There are plenty of studies that turned out not to be correct, because of some mistake in the study or the studies being too small or poorly controlled.

One useful way that scientists have to investigate the effects of nature/nurture is by focusing on twins – two people with the same genes, but different environments. One famous study by Robert Plomin looked at GCSE results in over 10,000 sets of twins. This number was probably large enough to account for confounding variables and give a fairly accurate result. Plomin found that your genes account for 58 per cent of how well you do in school, and your school itself accounts for only 42 per cent. This study is important because it suggests that your genetics and your environment are both important.

The Plomin study was based on exam performance, but there's a difference between exam performance and intelligence. And we aren't even sure how to define intelligence! You might have an excellent memory but no musical ability, loads of empathy but no

NATURE

NURTURE

problem-solving skills or artistic talent. These are difficult things to define and measure, and can be influenced by culture, education and experience. This is important, because in truth the difference between us all in intelligence is actually quite small.

BRAVE NEW WORLD

I love science fiction, because it looks to the future and makes us think about how the world would look if things changed slightly. One of my favourite science fiction books is Aldous Huxley's *Brave New World*, which basically ranked people from the smartest to the … Ah! Not smartest. At the top were the Alphas – a whole team of smarty-pants who could do algebra and play grade 8 piano and look after old people in their spare time. Then, at the bottom, came the Epsilons. Now, who on Earth wakes up one day and says, 'I want to be at the bottom of the pile'?

So, as *Brave New World* shows, if we do find a clear genetic cause for intelligence, it might be tricky. There is a real danger in saying 'This kid is smart, and this kid is not,' because we all want to feel we are good at something. Such statements can make us worried, anxious and very unhappy. But, on the other hand, knowing how intelligence works would help us to adapt teaching to each individual child. Why would you give a tennis racket to a child who had the right genes to be a mathematician?

And anyway, high intelligence doesn't guarantee that a person will be a high achiever. Irish economist David McWilliams once said that it's the messers down the back of the class who are likely to be the entrepreneurs and businesspeople.

And we can't forget about our environment. There is overwhelming evidence that poverty and lack of opportunities play a key role in success. Children with limited access to computers or books do worse in school (although that's not an excuse for that extra hour of Fortnite). Those who grow up in stimulating homes are much more likely to become entrepreneurs, leaders and artistic high achievers.

What seems to really matter is love. I'm not talking mushy stuff like poems and chocolates. I'm talking about having someone care for you. Research shows that if children under five don't get regular affection and good communication then they are held back in life. I'm sorry, but mammies rabbiting on at you all the time and hugging and kissing you at the school gates is actually making you better, smarter and happier ... I know, science ... what does it know?

A SWEET IDEA

Another key part of being successful is simply practice. You've all heard that 'practice makes perfect' and there is truth in that. Henry Shefflin didn't just pick up a hurl one day and have a go. King Henry practised, practised and when he was tired, he practised some more. The Williams sisters had training sessions that started as early as 6 a.m. and they sometimes had to return 500 volleys just to earn a rest for the evening. Of course, if any of us played tennis for hours and hours each day we might become champion tennis players too (or at a minimum go crazy).

This is where motivation comes in. What drives people like these to be the best? It seems to come down to grit and determination. Grit means having the willpower to see something through to the bitter end. It involves hard work and the ability to resist distraction. Never giving up, working hard and staying focused.

Some of that is about self-control. Scientists have poked people and entered millions and millions of pieces of data into their computers, and they say if you have better self-control you will be happier and more successful. If you can force yourself to do your homework instead of staying outside to play football, you will do better in life. It's a pain, but it's true.

Way back in the 1960s, a psychologist called Walter Mischel wanted to test the self-control of small children. He offered them a choice. He told them they could have one marshmallow right now, or if they held off for 15 minutes, they would get two marshmallows. He then went back to the kids years later, and he found that the children who held off for the two marshmallows and waited were more successful, more popular and healthier.

The ability to resist temptation and stay in control was a big reason for their success. It wasn't easy – the poor guys tried everything to distract themselves from the yummy sweet treats. They hid underneath tables, and they sang their favourite TV theme shows to themselves. Everybody wants the second marshmallow ... (Well, actually, I don't. I hate the things, but if it was a Twirl, I'd be in big trouble.)

This confirmed what psychologists have known for years – we can't control the world, but we can try to control how we think about it. Mischel thought that the important skill wasn't in forgetting about the marshmallow. Rather, the children *chose* to think about something else – they moved their attention elsewhere. This goes for studying instead of playing football, putting money in your piggybank and waiting for presents on Christmas morning. You need to be patient (I know, boring), to wait, to distract yourself and good things will come.

Better still, you need to be a dreamer. This sounds ridiculous, as people, especially teachers, might say, 'S/He is a daydreamer' and it is often thought to be something bad. But scientists have shown that many high achievers and creative people like writers, artists and musicians were just dreamers. Exam results and technical skills didn't really matter. They all had one thing in common – a strong sense of direction or purpose. Basically, they loved what they were doing, and they gave everything to it. Their lives weren't held back by biology but thrust forward by dreaming, dedication and practice.

So, we might not be able to escape our genetics, but with support, we can all learn patience, practice and purpose. Dare to dream. Climb every mountain. Wait 15 minutes for two marshmallows (or two Twirls) and dream the impossible dream. Sure, isn't that what our mammies have been teaching us forever? Good old mammies!

CHAPTER 6

THE

GOD

STUFF

THIS TOPIC HAS caused some of the biggest scraps ever, all over the world and for thousands of years. Entire wars were fought over it. And no, it's not about whether ketchup or mayo is better – it's about the big man upstairs, God.

The topic has always been polarised, with science and religion in opposite corners of the boxing ring. Any discussion usually ends unresolved with one or both people storming off to their room and slamming their door really, really hard. But we know all scientists must approach any topic with reasonableness, so let's give it a go.

We should start this whole debate by first saying that science isn't interested in why we're here. Like when you drift off and start asking yourself the big questions such as: 'Why do I exist? Is there someone identical to me in another solar system but they are 10 feet tall? Why does Mr Smyth always come back from lunch with biscuits in his teeth?' No, scientists are more interested in *how* we got here rather than why. Religion is mostly in the realm of *why* we came to be here. So, the two areas are completely separate. This is why we run into big, dramatic rockstar fights when we try to mix them together.

So, when it comes to the big questions, like our 'purpose' in life, the scientific answer isn't to annoy a sibling, or upset Miss Butler, or fart the entire alphabet in one go. No, science tells us that our purpose is to copy our magical DNA and pass it on to the next generation of 'you'. So that's it! Problem solved. Done and dusted. Let's all go home and have a KitKat.

Well … it's not so simple, obviously, because humans have believed in religion for as long as we have been humans. Might it be that faith in a higher power is a crucial part of being a human? Let's have a look at what science tells us about religious belief.

God ✔

@God

Following

I Love Justin Bieber

10:32 AM   OCT 2020

3,642 Retweets   5129 Likes

TRIBE TALK

Back before phones, computers and electricity (how did people even survive then?) we lived in small tribes, probably with no more than 250 people. Your tribe was made up of you, your relatives and in-laws. You all supported one another and avoided outsiders because they were a threat to your tribe. Scientists think that fear is why so many people nowadays are xenophobic – xenophobia is a fear of outsiders.

It is thought that in these small tribes, religion began as knowledge and wisdom passed down to the next generation. This advice probably took the form of moral guidance: look after your neighbour, don't cause problems, look after your family. This care for each other ensured that the copies of your DNA in your relatives would also get passed on.

Smart people in the tribe – the elders, or parents – would have come up with ways to make members behave, since there is a natural tendency for people to stray from the path and become what in Ireland are called 'messers'. One way to convince them is to tell them the wisdom has come from some kind of super-being. We then get the concept of a supernatural being providing advice. Would you be better behaved if you thought Captain America could pop in at any moment?

This is a common concept in many religions. By obeying and serving this powerful figure, your own relatives benefit and so the DNA passes on. There's always a risk of a few chancers not obeying these guidelines, but the risk is lessened because of the all-seeing father figure who can punish you. If the punishment doesn't materialise – if Captain America is nowhere to be seen – it is up to the wise elders to dish it out in the name of the divine power. This creates the need for religious leaders like priests, ministers, imams and gurus. All very understandable so far.

But here's where religion gets interesting. Scientific studies suggest that our religious belief may be in part genetic. You might actually carry in your body a gene variant (or most likely several) that may predispose you to being spiritual in certain circumstances. Some really interesting twin studies have compared twins brought up together in the same home with identical twins brought up in different circumstances. This allows researchers a way of looking at how much circumstances can alter the outcomes of genetically identical people. Recent studies in the USA suggest genes contribute about 40 per cent of a person's religious belief.

This set of genetic variants is likely to survive in a population because they will bring benefits. But only in a certain situation, for example the pre-agreed upon rules of a religion. If you are a person who is genetically disposed to hate cheese, you are more likely to survive and thrive in an environment where it is agreed that cheese is bad! (But let's be real, cheese is never bad.)

The survival of religion today in a modern world away from those original small tribes is intriguing. In fact, it mirrors science's survival of the fittest theory. You see, many studies show that religious people are healthier than non-believers and tend to share other personality traits such as the ability to get along well with others and be conscientious, work hard, be punctual and control impulsive behaviours. One theory goes that they have more moral support in that tribe than the non-believers on their own on the 'outside'.

Religions often focus on looking out for each other and social activities (such as religious ceremonies or chilli cookouts). We know social activity helps us a lot, decreasing the risk of heart disease, for example. And this kind of bonding is so much deeper than, say, the links between supporters of a football team, because it helps us deal with questions that are intrinsically human. Where did we come from? What happens after we die? These questions are in us because of our intelligence and capacity to ponder what might happen next – a defining trait of *Homo sapiens*.

PLASTIC BRAINS

Another piece in the puzzle is to do with the minds of children. The Jesuit priests ran the schools in Ireland for a long, long time. They have an old saying: 'Give me the boy of seven and I will give you the man'. They weren't saying that once you hit seven, that's it. The job's finished. No, they were referring to the plasticity of the brain at this stage. Plasticity doesn't mean that your head's filled with big blocks of LEGO. Rather, it refers to the brain's hunger and flexibility for ideas at this age. It is a perfect time to learn, explore and find out new stuff, but at the same time, learn the 'rules' that keep us safe.

This plasticity makes evolutionary sense. Imagine a child who is starting to explore the world outside their village. Maybe they see a really exciting-looking forest, full of dangerous things like snakes, bugs and bears. Time to explore! But their anxious father says, 'Don't go into that forest – there's a bogeyman in there.' And the child will believe him. They won't seek evidence for the bogeyman, because their brain is set up to receive and believe the information. They will find it very hard to escape this belief in the bogeyman and might even carry it with them for the rest of their life.

Think about it like the people who always end up dead or injured in horror movies. They will usually say and then do one of the following:

- 'That's the old Johnson place. It's haunted. Let's go in and have a look!'
- 'Right, we have a better chance if we split up when we go into the woods!'
- 'I heard a noise. I'm gonna go down to the basement!'

Your in-built evolutionary gut instinct tells you not to do any of the above if you hope to survive. Survival of the fittest again. Maybe people in horror movies were evolutionary dead ends in the first place!

CLOSING THE GAP

At times of threat, religion is very useful. Who hasn't been in a nightmare situation and thought something like: 'Dear God, if I get out of this one, I'll be good forever. I'll kiss my granny every night and rub her feet with that skin cream – well, I can't really follow through on the last one, but I'll do the rest!'

Religion has always thrived in places where there is great suffering. Poor people, or people in times of great trauma, are inclined to believe in a god more, possibly to give them hope and comfort. The problem has been, however, that such people are sometimes exploited by religious leaders who hold the money and the power. But religions also have great track records for charitable work and helping the vulnerable through poverty relief, education and healthcare. Their common message is tolerance, compassion and kindness – all good things.

Even though we said at the start of this chapter that the worlds of science and religion shouldn't mix, some say science is just another religion. If you scratch the surface, you can see some interesting things. Science and religion both regard people as the central focus of what they do. Religion reveres saints but people follow and worship people in the science world too. Think of the number of people sporting T-shirts with Einstein, Darwin or Newton on them. And both science and religion are bound by a code of ethics or rules.

Finally, science requires a faith of sorts. When a scientist is asked to explain big things like the Big Bang or superstring theory, most won't be able to unless they are specialists. They have to have faith that the other scientists know what they are actually talking about. The big difference, though, is that science has evidence to back up these explanations. As the astrophysicist Neil deGrasse Tyson has said, 'The good thing about science is that it's true whether or not you believe in it.'

CHAPTER 7

HERE'S A GOOD ONE: WHY DO WE LAUGH?

Y ES, IT COULD be the sight of your teacher bending down and ripping his trousers or watching your friend getting pooped on by a seagull, but what is certain is that we humans love to laugh. In fact, we top the laughter league and are way ahead of cheeky chimps and hilarious hyenas. But why do we laugh? Why do we find some things funny and other things not so much? What happens when we get the giggles? Laughing is complicated stuff.

THE BEST MEDICINE

So, what happens to our bodies when we laugh in the first place? Well, let's look at the 'belly' laugh (also known as a real laugh). When you belly laugh, your belly starts to vibrate, the muscles in your ribcage contract, and these contractions force air out of your body which ... hahaha! ... makes the sound of a laugh. (By contrast, what scientists call 'social laughing' doesn't have the same effects on the body. Social laughing is the sort of laughing that adults do at tea parties or outside of a school when they are chatting nicely while waiting for you. Awkward!)

In one scientific study, researchers showed a group of women a very funny movie, then a totally unfunny one. The unfunny one was probably a health and safety video that they show you in school all the time, with a title like HOW TO USE A TAP PROPERLY or SWITCH A LIGHT ON SAFELY. The scientists then strapped monitors to the women's bellies to count their belly laughs. The funny movie averaged 30 belly laughs per woman and the unfunny one averaged just 1 (which was probably because of a fart). The clever scientists then took a blood sample from each woman and looked at their immune system. They studied each woman's NK cells, or 'Natural Killer' cells, which don't actually kill people, but they do kill and fight off viruses. Yes, your body is full of natural killers ... cool or what? The scientists found that after laughing so much, the women's NK activity was greater. In other words, laughing can boost our immune systems. You can hear infections everywhere scream, 'Stop, you're killing me!'

The benefits of laughing don't end there. We have discovered it can help us in other ways. Laughing increases the flow of blood to your heart, which means a regular tee-hee-hee can help protect against heart disease. Even better, laughter has been classified as a form of exercise! In one scientific study, it was found that laughing 100 times was the equivalent of 10 minutes on a rowing machine or 15 minutes' cycling. So, the next time your PE teacher tells you to go for a run, tell them you're just gonna sit there and have a good laugh. Furthermore, laughing reduces our ability to feel pain, as well as reducing anxiety and fear. Is there nothing laughing can't do?

Scientists have also pondered on the physical nature of laughter – the sound we make and the way our mouths open. It may have come from threatening to bite, strange as that may seem. Although it's playful, the sound our mouths make sends out a signal of triumph and aggression. Smiling is also interesting in that regard. Babies will start to smile at around eight weeks of age, and this is a hard-wired response. We know it's not learned, because blind babies also smile. Smiling signals happiness with the situation, and pleasure. The mouth is closed, your teeth aren't bared and so you aren't a threat.

One psychologist has suggested that there are 19 different types of smile. Of these, only six occur when we're having a good time. The rest happen when we're in pain, embarrassed, uncomfortable, horrified or even miserable. A smile may mean contempt, anger or incredulity, that we're lying or that we've lost. Next time a photographer asks you to say cheese, you can ask them 'What kind?'

THE WORLD LAUGHS WITH YOU

Laughter is also a great way to strengthen social bonds. We laugh more in groups than we do when we are alone because laughter makes us feel more comfortable in a group and more relaxed. It's basically a clever technique humans use to make themselves seem harmless. Watch out for this next time you are with people: often your laughter is not at something funny, but rather is saying, 'I'm friendly, you don't need to fear me, please keep talking to me!'

And we all know that laughter is contagious. Have you ever caught a laugh from someone else simply because they are laughing and not because of what they are laughing at? And one bout of laughter will set us up to laugh again – this is why comedy shows have a warm-up comedian: once we start to laugh we are inclined to keep laughing.

Laughing brings us all together and helps us bond as a group.

Laughing also indicates status. For instance, people are more likely to laugh at their teacher or boss, even though most of the time these people are totally unfunny. It's our way of saying 'Like me ... don't punish me or fire me!'

Laughing our head off also relieves tension and dispels fear. It literally acts as a pressure valve and allows us to let off steam. We especially like to tell jokes in difficult situations and there is evidence that laughter is very common among surgeons, soldiers and undertakers – why did they put a padlock on the cemetery gates? People were just dying to get in there!

Then there's the phenomenon of 'corpsing'. No! You don't drop dead laughing, but you nearly do. You see, corpsing is basically an infectious outburst of laughter that you can't stop. It is usually found in a tense or stressful situation – like getting the giggles in church or an important exam – and the uncontrollable laughter relieves the tension of the situation. It might even happen when you're writing a serious book about science. Bahaha! Sorry.

THE PUNCHLINE

But what makes a joke actually funny? The danger in trying to explain humour is, as someone once said, that 'trying to explain why something is funny is like trying to dissect a frog. Nobody laughs and the frog dies.' Still, we must be brave. Science knows no boundaries, and as long as you get a laugh out of it, we'll be fine.

One thing that we always enjoy is toilet humour. Some of the oldest jokes in the world involve farts. So next time you let one rip in history class, you can tell your teacher that you're studying! Nonsense verse, clever wordplay or strange situations all amuse us. There is often a puzzle-solving aspect, where we're trying to figure out what happened and what might happen next.

Many comedians make jokes about the hassles of everyday life, and we find this funny because it reassures us that we're not alone in experiencing these embarrassing things. It makes us feel like we are all in the same boat. A lot of comedy also focuses on social awkwardness. This is to do with a fear of social exclusion that we all have – nobody wants to be the one with egg on their face!

We also love to use jokes to poke fun at or mock those in authority. That's why there are so many jokes about policemen, doctors, judges and politicians. These jokes make us feel better and more in control. They basically level the playing field and help us not feel threatened by those whom we see as having power over us.

Teacher: 'If I had six oranges in one hand and seven oranges in the other, what would I have?'
Student: 'Big hands!'

We can see the different types of humour in the development of children, who generate humour from a very early age. To begin with it's in things like peekaboo and funny body movements (falling and sticking legs in the air is hilarious to a one-

year-old). By the age of three, children will use objects in unexpected ways – putting underpants on their heads, for example. Although, to be fair, if an adult did this today you would probably still laugh!

TICKLE ME PINK

Have you ever heard the saying 'tickle me pink'? This gives you an idea what tickling and laughter does to the body. More blood floods around your body and you become pink-cheeked as you wriggle and writhe from all the laughter, struggling to breathe – you nearly die laughing! But you might be wondering about that age-old question 'Why can't we tickle ourselves?' Well, tickling actually activates the part of our brain that anticipates pain, so being tickled by someone else makes us jump and wriggle around. We see it as a threat, but when we do it to ourselves there is no threat because we know it is coming. So, it doesn't have the same effect.

It's even possible to wet yourself when laughing. Such an activity is not recommended here, but why does it happen? Well, when you start to laugh uncontrollably, you lose control of lots of things in your body from breathing to muscle control. As the pressure from laughing builds, the control of the bladder is lost and the flood gates literally open and whoosh! you're stuck in pee-pants central, which is not a good look. The same thing happens when you fart while laughing. The sphincter muscle in your bum gives way and some of the gas in your digestive tract is released as a fart. Hopefully, you only release the gas and nothing else! LMAO!

Another recent study asked a curious question: 'Can you tickle animals?' (Go on! Admit it, it's the first question you ask in the morning and the last thing at night!) Anyway, the only other animals that we know of that can be tickled are rats and apes. Koko, a western lowland gorilla who lived at the California-based Gorilla Foundation, was studied a lot. Researchers found she could be tickled and that she had a great sense of humour. Koko would often laugh when her keeper slipped on a banana skin (this is not a joke!).

Then there's the study into tickling rats, which found that when tickled, the rats made chirping noises that were the same as when they were playing together. The same scientists are currently spending their days tickling other animals to see if it makes them laugh.

And they said science was boring. Ha!

CHAPTER 8

THE
SOUND
OF
MUSIC

WHAT IS IT that makes us uniquely human? What sets us apart from other species? There may be many answers to this question, but a good possible answer is our love of music. Humans all over the world love it, across all communities and ethnic groups. And yet we're not really sure what it does for us as a species.

When scientists consider music, all kinds of questions come into their heads. You might wonder: Why can't they just listen to the music and enjoy it? Well, they can't. At least not all the time. This is the curse and the joy of being a scientist. We're always overthinking. But given how common music is in our daily lives, you might be surprised to hear that science has yet to come up with a convincing explanation of what it's all about.

Archaeologists tell us that our species has been enjoying it for a long time. One of the oldest agreed-upon musical instruments is a flute made from a mammoth bone dating to somewhere between 30,000 and 37,000 years ago, so music is clearly deep-seated in our psyche. The particular mammoth who gave his bone is long extinct, as are all his family and friends. But it seems that our ancestors loved the sound made by that punctured bone when someone blew into it. 'Go on, play "Baby Elephant Walk!"'

We have clear explanations for other pastimes. We play sport because it involves skills (throwing, hitting and moving as a team) that were crucial for our ancestors when they went on hunting expeditions or defended their tribe against other humans. We enjoy novels and films because they allow us to learn about the relationships crucial to our survival as a social species. But the enjoyment of music? This doesn't seem to help us do anything – or does it?

TUNING UP

Some of the music we listen to makes us happy and upbeat, and some music can leave us feeling down and blue. We've all danced around the room or sung into a hairbrush, while a slow, sad song can bring tears to our eyes.

In many ways, music is all about emotion. But as scientists, we can't leave it at that! And it turns out that there are still some scientific rules behind our love of a good tune. The notes of a musical chord will only sound good to us if their frequencies follow a clear mathematical relationship to one another. The science shows that for us to enjoy a melody, or sequence of notes, it must reveal a gradually emerging 'pattern' to the listener. Interestingly, this pattern that we start to like may then have a 'break' in it, and it is the break that we really, really love because it takes us by surprise or takes us off in another direction.

Different scientists have different theories as to why we love music so much. Some say it survives from a time before we had proper spoken language and was a cool and clever way of communicating across the valley. We could use these funny noises to tell others if we were sad, happy, angry or lonely.

Others say music could be a reminder of our 'intermediary' (middle) stage, where we used a range of chirps and hoots that animals use to communicate before we reached our current, very complex modern language stage.

This idea is backed up by the fact that animals also enjoy music, although animals prefer certain frequencies. Good old Labrador dogs, for example, have similar vocal ranges to us humans and can make all sorts of noises that sound like they are singing. Better still, they can be classed as the animal world's musical snobs and much prefer to relax with a sophisticated evening of classical music like Mozart, and they become quite agitated when they hear the noisy din of heavy metal (rock on, dawg!).

Funnily, cats aren't interested in music at all and will give absolutely no response to it until it is played at a frequency in their vocal range. Then it's just puuuurrrrrfect! In Thailand, there is an elephant orchestra – a team of elephants who are musically trained. They have learned to play instruments in different keys and are reported to enjoy playing best when the instruments are in tune. When music is played to cows, they even produce more milk.

OK, getting back to humans. We know there are people on Earth who have absolutely no musical appreciation. In fact, around 1 in 25 of us has a condition called 'amusia', which isn't very amusing at all. Its effects range from tone deafness (the inability to hear different tones and pitches in music) through to a complete lack of appreciation for music. Some people are born with amusia, and others get it following a head injury.

BOOGIE BENEFITS

Music certainly appears to be good for humans, even if we don't fully understand how. More than 400 studies have been carried out and the overwhelming conclusion is that music is good for our immune systems, lowers the stress hormone cortisol and is better at regulating our stress than medication.

Listening to music can even be classed as a form of exercise. Yes, you see, scientists have used scanners and discovered that when listening to music, a part of the brain called the arcuate fasciculus lights up. This means this part of the brain burns more glucose, just as you would by walking or running.

This is all superb stuff, but now it gets a bit freaky ... studies have shown that if a group of people are listening to background music, say in an elevator or hotel lobby, their heart rates will all synchronise with one another until the entire group is at the exact same heart rate – even if you are all complete strangers!

Music can bring us all together into one big community, even

when we don't know anyone. Think about it: there is a reason why armies have bands and march into battle to the beat of a drum. There is a reason why we sing at the top of our voices at a concert next to thousands of strangers, and there is a reason why we sing our favourite anthems at large sporting events like a football match. These events bring us together in a collective and bind us to one another. In addition, such events become an emotional and physical experience that unites us. Quite simply, as one famous football chant goes: 'You'll never walk alone'.

Singing in groups seems especially good for humans. The USA alone has 28.5 million people who sing in a quarter of a million choirs across the country. The research shows that being in a choir is good for both our physical and mental health. Belting tunes out loud helps our breathing and standing shoulder to shoulder with our friends makes us feel good. Choir members have what scientists call 'stress-free zones' – they have to concentrate so hard on the music and their technique, they literally forget about their worries. They are also learning new songs, harmonies and tempos, which are all food for the brain. And elderly residents of care homes who sing together regularly have less anxiety and depression, but why?

Well, the act of singing releases happy hormones called endorphins. Better still, singing in front of an audience has been shown to build self-confidence, with long-lasting effects. The same pattern has also been discovered in birds. When male songbirds sing, their brains' pleasure centres light up, but interestingly, this only happens when the females are present. If the males sing alone, it makes no difference whatsoever.

This leads us nicely to the next benefit of music. It can actually make you smarter! Research has shown that playing music in the background can improve how you learn. One study showed that those learning a foreign language with music playing learned 8.7 per cent more words in the same time span as those who didn't. These findings are similar to the so-called 'Mozart Effect', which showed that listening to Mozart improved people's test performance. So, turn up the tunes while you ace that homework!

WEAPONISED BEATS

I'm afraid it's not all 'Don't worry, be happy' – there can be downsides. All across the globe, music has been and continues to be used as a punishment – especially targeting teens! In the town of Rockdale near Sydney in Australia, the music of the singer Barry Manilow is blasted outside shops to prevent teenagers loitering there. They definitely won't be singing his hit 'Turn the Radio Up'. A judge in the USA ordered teenagers who were charged with antisocial behaviour to repeatedly listen to the theme tune from the children's TV programme *Barney & Friends*. There is also a device called Teen Away, which generates high-frequency noises that people over about the age of 30 can't hear. Whether it actually works is another matter. However, teens are also known to use this different perception of frequencies to their advantage – they can use a ring tone that their parents can't hear. Shhh – I didn't tell you that.

MEDICAL MUSIC?

One final bone of contention (get it?) is about the use of music in operating theatres. As far back as 100 years ago, an American surgeon wrote to the *Journal of the American Medical Association* describing the benefits of music in the operating room. Indeed, the link between music and medicine goes back much further than that. As far back as 6,000 years ago, harp players were hired as payment for medical services. The Greeks even made Apollo their god of healing and music.

The benefits in medical settings seem clear, not least for the patient – it has been shown to be more calming than medication, even for those on ventilators in intensive care. Then there's the effect on surgeons and the medical staff. A whopping 72 per cent of medical operations are carried out with music playing and 80 per cent of staff said it was beneficial in team building, reducing anxiety and, best of all, improving the surgeon's performance. Some research shows that the music helps the surgeon focus on the task and reduces muscle fatigue. However, some worry that the music is a

distraction, and this does seem to be the case with trainees. It also increases what one study called 'general irritation', which can't be a good thing in the operating theatre.

The final question then must be: If you are going to play music in an operating theatre, what would you have on your playlist?

TOP 5 TO PLAY

'Medicine' by The 1975 or Harry Styles

'Doctor Feel Good' by Travie McCoy

'Just Like a Pill' by Pink

'Getting Better' by The Beatles

'Stayin' Alive' by The Bee Gees

TOP 5 TO PROBABLY AVOID

'Heart Attack' by Demi Lovato

'(I Just) Died in Your Arms' by Cutting Crew

'Stitches' by Shawn Mendes

'Bleeding Love' by Leona Lewis

'Another One Bites the Dust' by Queen

CHAPTER 9

TICK TOCK, YOUR BODY CLOCK

DID YOU KNOW that your body has its own clock? I don't mean that you're a walking, talking Big Ben or have a cuckoo popping out of your forehead every hour, but you do have a clock inside you that divides up your body's essential activities. It has an annoying in-built alarm that tells you when to eat, when to sleep and when to grow. I know, I have just described your mum, who tells you when and where and how to do absolutely everything in your life, but what are you gonna do?

The division of activities makes perfect sense. After all, not everything can happen at once or your life would be a complete mess. You can't fall asleep and be awake at the same time. You can't eat a big meal and work hard at the same time, and just like nature's own clock, it can't be day and night at the same time. As a result, your body has an in-built schedule for different programmes to do different things at just the right time. Scientists say these 'rhythms' regulate everything from your stomach to intestines from your brain activity to cell repair.

Practically all animals on Earth have this internal daily planner, but the 'clocks' of other animals appear more flexible than humans' and allow them to adapt to their environments. Unlike our association with light and dark cycles, animals operate a little differently. For example, *Platynereis dumerilli* is a marine worm that doesn't follow the sun but rather the rise and fall of the moon in what is called a lunar clock. Similarly, another ocean goer, the speckled sea louse, works between tidal rhythms in what is called a tidal clock.

A favourite of the honeybee is the social clock, which isn't the same as your older sister's social life. The bees adjust their clocks to complete foraging shifts, while nurse bees stop their rhythm so that they can give constant care to their new baby larvae in the hive. Nurse bees, eh? And you thought they were all just stripy, buzzy weirdos who love sitting on flowers all day.

A DAY IN THE LIFE

The scientific term for how our bodies change over the course of the day is 'circadian rhythm' – 'circadian' meaning 'about a day'. Let's look at the typical events that happen in our bodies over the course of a day. Between 6 a.m. and 9 a.m., most people wake up. We are of course excluding that strange creature, the teenager, who has very different sleeping patterns from others! But for most people, certain changes to our hormones and blood pressure get us ready for the day ahead and prepare us for activities.

Between 9 a.m. and 12 noon, the stress hormone cortisol peaks, which gives our brains a boost of alertness. We tend to be most productive at work or school before lunch, when our short-term memory is at its best. Our stomachs create digestive juices, and we feel hungry because of the release of hormones that poke the parts of our brains that say 'Hey! You're feeling a bit peckish.' Between 12 noon and 3 p.m., our bellies will be full of food, if you haven't accidentally left your lunchbox behind on the kitchen counter. AGAIN.

And, of course, once we've eaten, we experience that familiar early afternoon slump, the post-lunch dip. Yaaaawn. Our alertness takes a nosedive at this time, we feel sleepy and there are more accidents on the roads. Some cultures take a power nap at this point of the day, called a siesta. But between 3 p.m. and 6 p.m. our body temperature rises slightly, our hearts and lungs work better, and our muscles are stronger, so now is a good time for a game of football.

Between 6 p.m. and 9 p.m. you are ready for dinner. But don't leave this too late, as the way the body handles food changes as we get closer to night-time. We are more likely to store food as fat, so it's a bad idea to eat at night. This is in part because we are more active during the day and burn it off, but it also appears to be due to storage of fat being more active at night.

Then, at bedtime, our bodies make our own sleeping tablet in the form of melatonin. When our eyes detect the dimming light, melatonin is made by our brains, which makes us fall asleep. When we travel across time zones, melatonin gets made at a different time compared with local time and so we fall asleep at the wrong time – this is what we call jet lag. Blue light, the type of light emitted from computer screens or smartphones, suppresses melatonin, so it is not a good idea to look at devices at night-time. Turn off that tablet and go to sleep!

STAGES OF SLEEP

Every one of us needs sleep, because without it we become irritable, crave sweet or fatty foods and go a bit loopy. A lack of sleep, or insomnia, can be bad for us and may be linked to diseases like Alzheimer's disease. It can also cause other nasty things, like weaker bones and cravings for junk food.

And, importantly, a lack of sleep will eventually kill you. This is true – mice kept awake will die after a few days. It's not really clear what they die from (other than their brains and hearts ceasing to work), so we can't find out what sleep is actually for, other than keeping us from becoming very irritable and ultimately dying. Which are pretty important things to avoid, to be fair. (Not sure what they used to keep the mice awake – perhaps a foghorn or tiny cups of coffee!)

Our brains go through five stages once we lie down for a snooze, and you can pass through each of these stages four to five times a night. The first stage is a light, relaxed state where a fart or a burp would wake you up. In the second stage, things slow down even more, but you're not yet fully asleep. It is here that you start to dream about winning the World Cup or marrying a prince, or maybe doing both at the same time. In this state, you are open to suggestion, and this is where hypnotists famously make their money. When some people are hypnotised, they can be lulled into this same sleep state. That's why hypnotists can get your teacher in front of a room full of people and make them think they're a leprechaun or make your granny think she is a world champion boxer.

By stage three, your heart rate starts to slow, and in stage four, some people sleepwalk or bed wet at this point (but we don't fully know why). Stage five is the final stage, and it is called the REM or Rapid Eye Movement stage. That's because your eyeballs dart around like you are playing some demented video game. You are now in deep sleep!

There are several theories for our sleep patterns. Some scientists say it is an evolutionary survival trait from when we lived in caves. At night, humans would be more vulnerable to attacks or to being eaten by predators. So, a caveperson finds a nice, warm, semi-detached cave in the leafy suburbs with good roads and good cave schools. Caveperson stays very still at night, so they survive and avoid becoming a cave meal-deal.

A second sleep theory looks at energy conservation. Hunting is more difficult at night. We fall asleep when it's dark, which saves us having to hunt down and eat a McMammoth. The evidence shows that during sleep our energy use drops by 10 per cent. Evolution could work its magic again and randomly select this trait, providing an advantage over those who don't sleep.

The third theory (I hope I haven't put you to sleep at this stage) is the restorative theory, where the body repairs and rejuvenates you while you snore like a baboon. Your brain clears out all the debris your body has built up during the day. Think of a big city at night, when the refuse lorries and the road sweepers get the place ready for the next, busy day. Your body is just the same, only less smelly than an old bin down beside the fish market. Sleep is all about clean-up time.

When we are young, sleep appears to have an especially important role in brain development. Infants will sleep for up to 14 hours per day, and at least half that time is spent in REM sleep. Lots of electrical activity happens, like a building site where the electrics are being installed and tested. Children from 6 to 13 years old need about 10 or 11 hours of sleep a day.

An International Bedroom Poll has been done (now there's a great title for a survey) across several countries. The USA and Japan have it worst, sleeping on average 40 minutes less than people in other countries. The Japanese average 6 hours and 22 minutes, while the Americans average 6 hours and 31 minutes. Germans, Mexicans and Canadians report the longest time asleep, with over seven hours in each country. Every country reports sleeping more at weekends, with an average of an extra 45 minutes on days they do not work. This is why waking your parents up early on weekends is a very dangerous thing to do!

RESETTING OUR CLOCKS

Space travel is an area where our rhythms are tested to the max. The astronauts on the International Space Station put their body clocks through a gruelling regime, which includes everything from weightlessness and G-force to the way they have to poop and pee up there. In addition, they witness a whopping 16 sunsets and sunrises every single day. So, specialised lighting that mimics the Earth's 24 hour daylight cycle is being tested. This has the potential to reduce health issues as well as improve mood and keep the astronauts in peak condition. Otherwise, 16 sunrises and sunsets a day would really mess with your head!

Back on Earth, we need to keep this in mind too. Recent research shows that we may be messing with nature and our bodies by the way we live our lives. Whatever way your body clock is set up, maybe it's about time you changed a few things in your daily schedule to see if your body and brain could benefit. Technology has a lot to answer for when it comes to getting too little sleep. For example, do you struggle to sleep if you've just been gaming for a long time? Or if you have been on a tablet or your phone? How about if you leave a light on?

You won't want to hear this but before bed, turn down the music and the blinding lights, put away the PlayStation and turn off the phone ... I said, TURN IT OFF!

DID YOU KNOW?

Some people sleep with their eyes entirely open at night. How freaky would that be? Thankfully, this horror show is very rare, and doctors call it nocturnal lagophthalmos, but I call it 'nocturnal big scary eyeball monster on the other side of the room-ism'.

DID YOU KNOW?

A few thousand years ago, if you ground your teeth at night, doctors thought you were trying to speak with ghosts. Their solution? You had to take a human skull to bed with you and either kiss it or lick it several times a night. 'I'm prescribing you a course of skull licking. Sadly, we're out of strawberry and apple skulls. You'll just have to make do with a manky, dead and decaying flavour.'

DID YOU KNOW?

Sea otters hold hands with one another when they sleep. They do so to make sure they don't drift away from each other. Ahh! Isn't that sweet! Each one looks after the otter one ... get it? The 'otter' one! I'm wasted here on you guys.

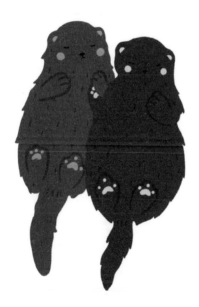

CHAPTER 10

OUR

TRICKY

RELATIONSHIP

WITH

FOOD

F OOD, GLORIOUS FOOD! Since life on Earth began, it has needed nutrients. All living things have to eat if they, well, want to live. We eat to give our bodies the energy they need to do work. Food is the fuel we put in our tanks, but also to build and maintain the parts we need to keep the car running. Sound fairly straightforward? Sadly, that's not the case.

The study of food is full of bad science, and equally full of controversy. And today, our relationship with food has become a little rocky and problematic. (Using the word 'relationship' to describe how you and your food interact might seem a bit much. But you have to admit that there have probably been occasions when you have spoken to your food, with a line like 'OMG! You look soooo good.')

The developed world is suffering from an obesity epidemic. Even here in Ireland, 25 per cent of people are classed as overweight or obese, and that figure looks set to rise. Being overweight brings many health problems such as heart disease, diabetes and an increase in the likelihood of getting cancer. Governments all over the world are trying to stem the tide of obesity, with everything from decreasing the fat content in processed foods to placing a tax on sugar.

STONE AGE APPETITE

One of the simple problems is the way our bodies have evolved – you still live in a Stone Age body. By that I don't mean you have long, matted hair filled with lice, a scrawny beard and hairy armpits! No, your body evolved for the conditions it found about 200,000 years ago, when your teacher was born. Food back then was hard to find. You had to go looking for it, hunt it, kill it, cook it, then eat it. You couldn't pick up the phone and ask for a delivery of super-mega-sized pizzas with garlic bread, sides of chicken and wedges and a gallon of cola!

As a result, when you did hit the Stone Age mega-meal jackpot, you had to eat as much as you could so that when you were full, some of that energy was stored up as fat in your body. Our bodies are amazing at storing fat for fuel. The energy we release when we burn fat is incredible – it is at least 10 times more than the energy released when we burn the same amount of sugar. So, we store fat for a rainy day when we are starving.

Fast forward to today, and the truth is that we are rarely ever starving. Food is everywhere we look and too much of it will make us obese. Back in the good old days, you just slipped your feet into a pair of the newest Nike Air Max Cave Runners, grabbed your spear and chased dinner for a day or two. Sometimes, over great distances. This meant cave-you was getting lots of exercise as well as eating less than we do today.

Scientists call our lack of exercise a 'sedentary lifestyle', where we sit in one place for long periods, usually not doing much more than gaming, watching TV or playing on our phones. Too much food and too little exercise is working against us.

Of course, in some parts of the world, there is still not enough food, which may happen when crops fail due to drought, pests or too much moisture. Climate change is worsening these food problems, causing extreme weather events that destroy farmland. But the problem can also come from the uneven distribution of natural resources in a country, and by human institutions, such as governments. However, in most of the Western world, we are indeed in the land of milk and honey ... and sugar ... and milkshakes ... and cookies ... mmmm!

TASTY HORMONES

But is it really as simple as 'we eat too much and move too little'? Some recent science tells us other elements are at work. Scientists have identified hormones that control our appetite, direct us to certain foods and can act as an off switch that basically screams, 'Stop eating now!'

Two really important hormones have names that sound like dwarves from *The Lord of the Rings* – Leptin and Ghrelin. Leptin was a big breakthrough. It is mainly made by fat cells and helps regulate the energy balance in your body by stopping you from feeling hungry. Scientists got very excited by little leptin and thought they could help people who were eating too much, but like all science, it was much more complex than that.

How leptin was discovered all comes down to mice. Scientists were studying mice that ate practically everything in their way and became obese. In 1990, they found the gene that was responsible for making leptin (which is Greek for 'thin', by the way), but because the gene was broken, the mice were missing the leptin they needed to tell them to stop eating. When it's made normally, it says, 'Stop looking for food because you have plenty of fat in storage.' So, can we use leptin as a treatment for obesity? Sadly, we can't have our cake and eat it – further work is needed before we can understand how leptin actually works in our bodies.

But this work on leptin later led to the discovery of a second hormone that affects appetite called ghrelin. If your body has low levels of leptin, due to low stores of fat, then a trigger is set off for the release of ghrelin into the body. Ghrelin is a very clever piece of evolution that makes you feel hungry. When you see an ad for a gooey, cheesy pizza, and you feel hungry, it is probably ghrelin that is making you want that food. Also, the evidence shows that when you are stressed, ghrelin is made. This might explain the need to eat in stressful situations. Think about it: 'Give me that cake. I have a maths test later,' or 'I can't cope. Aunt Mabel's coming to collect me. Pass me that chocolate biscuit!'

Another interesting hormone, whose name doesn't quite have the same ring as leptin and ghrelin, is FGF21, which sounds more like a fighter jet. FGF21 is made after we have eaten sugar and its job is to try to regulate how much sugar we stuff down our cake hole. If we are one of the lucky ones and make lots of FGF21, then we are less likely to run up to a vending machine and start licking it, hugging it and telling it we love it. For those of us who have less of it, the temptation is too strong, and we are probably a regular, drooling against the sweetshop window.

What do we know about these cravings? We all have these, and they can suddenly jump up on you. Seemingly out of nowhere you will have a craving for some salt-and-vinegar crisps or a bag of toffees. Some will crave a type of food that others won't like at all. What is it that gives us these appetites? Preferences might be formed in part while we are still in our mother's wombs. A fan of carrots, for example, will give birth to one (a fan that is, not a carrot). And all mammals have a craving for sweet things, perhaps because it is the main taste in their mother's milk.

One possible cause here is the rush that we get in our brains when we eat food. We basically go all warm and fuzzy. Dopamine is the chemical responsible for this feeling. Research that scanned the brains of teenagers just after eating ice cream found no brains present ... joking! Those who had ice cream as an occasional treat showed huge brain activity, but those who had it all the time had much lower signals. This showed they had become desensitised to the dopamine, which means they would need to eat more to get the same effect. So, your mam was right again – no ice cream sundae for breakfast.

PSYCHIC SALADS

The psychology behind how and what we eat can be pretty strange. Some clever scientists have discovered that if you are shown a picture of a certain food, you actually go off that food – at least for a short while. This might be so that you don't eat too much of the same thing and miss out on important nutrients. Evolution again.

Some of the other discoveries are odd, to say the least. It seems that if we eat food off a round plate, it tastes sweeter than if it were on square plate. If you eat with a copper spoon, it can make the food taste bitter. Strawberry mousse, it seems, tastes 10 per cent sweeter on a white plate compared with other colours, while coffee tastes less bitter if it is served in a transparent blue glass … Who knew, eh? And there's more: red soft drinks will be rated sweeter and yellow ones will be rated as sourer in taste. An experiment by an American drinks company bombed when the makers came up with a colourless cola called 'Tab Clear', even though it had the exact same taste as the regular version!

You see, a lot of our taste involves other senses: our eyes, nose and ears. That doesn't mean you start stuffing carrots and peas in your earholes and nostrils or pouring custard into your eyeballs. No, that would be madness and rather messy! But there are other ways to test this out.

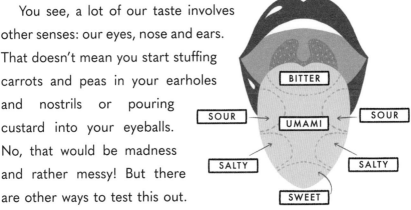

For instance, try to eat some mint while pinching your nose. There will be no real taste until you un-pinch your nose and the mint sensation flows to your brain.

Part of the reason for this is that you only have five types of receptors for taste – salt, sweet, bitter, sour and savoury (also called umami) – while the nose has thousands of receptors for smell. Then there are other amazing factors at work that posh foodies are discovering. For example, they have discovered that lighting in a restaurant plays a key role, with green and red lighting adding fruitiness to red wine. Under blue lights, men actually eat less ... Crazy!

Then there's the other impacts on the eyes – a psychologist found that diners preferred their salads if they looked like a painting by an artist called Kandinsky. If you've seen a Kandinsky, both the painting and the salad look like they've been in a fight with a blender. And yet, this is the beauty of taste – or lack of it. People will pay for all sorts of things in restaurants. The coolest hipsters are paying a fortune to eat their dinners off stuff you might dig out of a skip like house bricks and old wooden planks or dog bowls. With that in mind, I'm off to lunch in my favourite wheelie bin, which is positioned beneath a dim streetlight, with a Kandinsky hanging in it, to eat a lovely cold soup out of an old sock.

FUTURE FOOD

What might the future look like for food? Maybe the answer is in synthetic meat. Scientists have figured out how to grow meat from a single cell in a lab. This cuts out all the resources needed to feed, farm and process animals. One reason to decrease meat production is to save the planet. Meat production is a huge cause of greenhouse gases. In Ireland, one-third of our greenhouse gases come from farm animals belching methane, which is eight times as damaging as carbon dioxide.

Another reason to eat lab-grown meat is that synthetic burgers are a lot less fattening, which might keep us healthier. A third is that synthetic meat might eventually be easier and cheaper to produce, which could help us address hunger in developing countries. But the problem might be with the customers – studies show that most people don't like the thought of eating meat that is grown in a lab. How would you feel about eating a frankenfurter?

Another option is to look to insects as a source of food, as they are high in protein and easy to 'farm'. Some cultures already eat beetles, caterpillars, bees, wasps and ants. Are you looking forward to chowing down on a grasshopper sandwich? Mmm ... the future is crunchy.

DID YOU KNOW?

The idea of eating any kind of liver probably makes you feel sick to your stomach. The native Inuit peoples of the high Arctic are experts, and have long been wary of eating the polar bear's liver. The Inuit know that polar bears' liver contains an extremely high concentration of Vitamin A due to their rich diet of fish and seals. But the European explorers arrived without a clue and happily munched their way through the stuff, causing vitamin A poisoning, known as acute hypervitaminosis A. This results in vomiting, hair loss, bone damage and even death. Won't be ordering that tonight!

CHAPTER 11

SO, YOU WANNA BE A SUPERHERO?!

ALL OF US mere mortals would love to have a superpower, like super strength, super speed or the ability to fly. But even though comic books and movies might still be just fantasy, the real science is heading in this direction. Yes! The signs are that science fiction may, one day, be science fact. This is down to recent advances in genetic engineering, especially a technique called CRISPR (which isn't a reference to your hair, chips or favourite snack). The reality is that one day we might create disease-resistant humans through our ability to correct faulty genes before they are even born. Humans with super vision. Humans with super strength ... Think of real-life Fionn MacCumhaill or your friendly neighbourhood Spiderman. How could this be possible?

PADDLING IN THE GENE POOL

The truth is, we don't need that much technology to make a superhuman. We have been naturally trying to do this since the beginning of time. You see, we are programmed to seek out the best possible mate we can find and search for traits that will make us strong and invincible. We are really keen on certain things like intelligence, shiny hair, a big mouth full of teeth and breathing ... breathing is important!

But as we speak, there are companies that are already in the business of building super humans. For example, one such organisation called 23andme is working on something called FTIC or the Family Trait Inheritance Calculator. This invention uses genetic and computer technology to allow hopeful future parents to pick certain characteristics they might want their child to have … think of the big mouth full of teeth! In fact, many other companies like this already exist. There are vast databases that allow mothers to find out the eye colour, the height, the intelligence – as well as the wealth and family background – of a sperm donor, and it's big business.

Some feel we can improve other human characteristics that affect our personality, like your sense of humour or how affectionate you are. Fancy a designer baby? Are we nearly at Gucci Gucci Goo? Well, we have come a long way already. Imagine queuing in a waiting room to order a brand-spanking new human … I want a child that:

- Has the brain of Albert Einstein
- Smells like strawberry ice cream
- Can run like a cheetah
- Laughs at my jokes and
- Never farts

We might laugh, but the science tells us that such a world is not too far away. CRISPR already allows us to fix the gene linked to heart disease before you are even born.

A word of warning, though: this brave new world could be dangerous, and important questions need to be asked because it sets up a difference between the 'haves' and 'have-nots'. If you're rich, you can afford it; if you're poor, you can't. The ethics of using

CRISPR on humans – whether it's right or wrong – have been hotly debated, and it has been banned in many countries. International guidelines say that humans shouldn't be altered using CRISPR. The fear is that once it starts, it won't stop, and the population of the Earth will be dramatically changed. For the first time ever, there is a species on Earth (i.e. us) who can tamper with genetics. And we all know from movies what happens when advanced technology like this gets into the wrong hands ...

One fine day, purely in the interests of research for this book (and assuming mine aren't the wrong hands!), I had my DNA tested. Guess what I found out? Well, basically, I am a genetic disaster, to be honest. I am ...

- Hypersensitive to the blood-thinning drug Warfarin, which stops dangerous blood clots
- Prone to Norovirus – the winter vomiting bug
- At a high risk of blindness in old age

If you combined all these factors to create my superhero mantra, then I guess it would be 'Here he comes to save the day, it's the short-sighted vomiting clot man!' Evildoers will be quaking in their boots.

ANIMAL ALTERATIONS

As well as humans, we can also mess around with the animal world. We have altered dogs, goats and monkeys, but it is in pigs where the most progress has been made. I'm not telling porkies! We can make fat pigs, thin pigs, big pigs and small pigs. You can even buy a pet called a micro-pig, which is six times smaller than a normal pig.

'Pig kidney' might sound like a disgusting dish that a really snobby relative might order at a fancy restaurant that costs about 80 squilllion euro (and even then you still need a Mars bar after you've finished), but in reality, we are very close to using pig's organs in humans. This would be brilliant for saving lives and addressing the shortage in transplant organs we currently have. Basically, we are close to an organ drivethrough that fixes all our ills: 'I'd like to order two new legs, a kidney and a diet coke, please.'

Further still, in this Willy Wonka land of scientific advancements, we humans can boast to our friends that we have made goats with longer hair to produce more cashmere wool ... Great! Even more itchy jumpers and scarves from Granny at Christmas. Yet, more seriously, we can fix mosquitoes so that they aren't able to breed, then send them out into the world. This means that we could soon wipe out the disease malaria, which currently kills millions of people each year.

SUPER SKILLS

Doctors, scientists and researchers have brought us to this amazing point. They are, after all, really clever humans. In the past, doctors would normally have studied sick people to find out new cures but, recently, the clever clogs have changed their approach. Now they are looking at people who *aren't* sick – people who are infected with a disease or virus but who never get ill. These are the people who have defied all logic and defeated their own biology. By studying these people scientists might be able to learn how to help other people avoid illness.

Sporting skill has also been studied. Scientists are trying to help our muscles work better. This might be used to strengthen muscles in the elderly or to invent new treatments for muscle-wasting diseases. But if we could intervene, would we want to make a superhuman who had huge sprinting abilities or endurance? Athletes from East Africa have long been known to be superb performers over long distances, but we have yet to find a large part of the genetic basis for sports performance. A protein was found that can generate muscle mass. When this was engineered into a mouse, the mouse had muscles that were three times stronger than an ordinary mouse's. They had become Supermouse!

Scientists have had fun wondering whether it might actually be possible to make superheroes like in the legends. The Irish hero Fionn MacCumhaill could throw rocks the size of the Isle of Man. In the USA, comic books and Hollywood have come up with (fictional) ways to give humans superpowers. We've all seen the movie where a scientist is working in the lab late one night. An unfortunate accident happens, with some science attached to it – exposure to some toxic chemical or being bitten by a radioactive spider – and hey presto, we get the Hulk or Spiderman.

Superheroes often start off as scientists. Bruce Banner, who became the Incredible Hulk, is a good example. They are inclined to be handsome, rugged types, which immediately puts us on alert that this can't be true, given that, as we all know, scientists are awkward wimps with glasses and buck teeth, who spend all their time in the lab doing incredibly boring things. Is there any likelihood that we could turn scientists into superheroes (which, of course, they are already)?

Creating someone with Superman's powers would be impossible. His ability to lift heavy objects is put down to gravity being much stronger on his home planet of Krypton. His ability to fly comes down to willpower alone, which sadly will never be achieved. (Although, as writer Douglas Adams once said, the knack to flying is to throw yourself at the ground – and miss).

With Spiderman, we are on slightly more solid ground. Peter Parker is a human who is transformed by the bite of a spider that has been exposed to radiation. This might have changed the DNA in the spider, with the venom that it injected into Peter then changing his own genes. Maybe the writer of Spiderman foresaw CRISPR! He has a super-grip and is able to walk up walls and across ceilings. Insects can do this in part by having specialised hairs at the base of their feet that allow them to grip. And what about the web he weaves? A spider's web is made of silk, which is rich in a protein called keratin. It has huge strength, so it might even be possible for Spiderman to catch criminals with the silk he fires out, and  string them up. Scientists are currently examining the silk spiders make to see what they can learn from it in order to make stronger bags and other materials.

And what about his special Spidey Sense? Spiders do have special hairs called setae, which are connected directly to the spider's nervous system and can detect changes in air pressure and temperature. Perhaps Spiderman has these too, and can detect changes in the air, which gives him super hearing abilities. So, who knows, if we looked to the animal kingdom for inspiration, we could perhaps make a Spiderman.

The Incredible Hulk also draws on some real science. In the recent version, Bruce Banner's father, who is tampering with DNA, changes his own, which is then passed down. Again, did the writers see the origins of CRISPR? Bruce then is exposed to gamma rays – a very high-energy form of radiation. This leads to further changes. This could all build up muscle mass. But the business of suddenly building such mass is too far-fetched, as it takes years for these transformations to occur. So, it's back to the gym for now!

DID YOU KNOW?

If we take a look at Denmark, we could learn a thing or two about making superhumans. There, they are not only environmentally friendly, but since 2006 they have been recycling people! Yes, Denmark's 31 crematoriums have managed to recycle and sell more than 1.6 tonnes of knee and hip replacements ... Gives a whole new meaning to 'she's got her granny's knees'!

CHAPTER 12

ROBOFUTURE: ARE ROBOTS COMING TO SAVE US OR ENSLAVE US?

HOW MANY MOVIES have you seen where a robot goes mad and turns on the humans who created it? And the hero has to shut it off, before saying something cool like 'Compute that' or 'You shouldn't have pushed my buttons' or 'I never liked heavy metal anyway'? People have been making worrying predictions about robots and AI – artificial intelligence – for a very long time. Things like:

- Robots will become more intelligent than us!
- Robots will take all our jobs!
- Robots will take over the world!

Well, guess what, at least some of this is coming true. Should we be afraid? Very afraid? Or should we embrace all of this? We might even become freer and happier as a result.

ROBOCOPS OR ROBOSHOPS?

Many repetitive jobs have been replaced by machines, like in shops where you can pay at self-service checkouts. How many times a day do you think a human could say 'item removed from bagging area' before exploding from boredom? Scientists haven't yet managed to create a robot that can get bored – which is good news for us. We already see robots doing household chores. The vacuuming Roomba or window-washing Windoro are more and more common. There are also stain-removing robots, who might finally be able to get that chewing gum out of the carpet.

In Beijing, there are more than 20 bookshops that have no human staff. These automated bookshops are staffed only by robots and are open 24 hours a day. The robots give customers book recommendations and other advice. Roboshops are now opening up all over the city. This could be the normal shopping experience for us all very soon. Might buying new socks be easier and less stressful if it was just you and Shop-Bot?

One company called Silicon Valley Robotics has a robot that will greet guests before checking them into their hotel room. They say people prefer dealing with a robot than a human at a time when they might be tired or simply want to relax. Laugh if you like, but the very smile on your face is next. The Chinese are developing ATMs that recognise you by your face, which will allow you to 'smile and pay'.

Strange developments are also happening in the worlds of entertainment, music and art. 'Surely not,' you may well think. 'How could a robot replace Bono or Adele?' Well, you simply build a hologram – a type of image made with lasers that can make an image look solid. This happened at a concert in Las Vegas in 2012. The rapper, Tupac Shakur performed as a totally lifelike hologram … even though he had been dead for 16 years. ABBA are on the road virtually as a band of holograms … Mamma Mia! Think of the possibilities – future generations could buy a ticket for concerts performed by The Beatles or Elvis. Your parents might finally stop saying 'Music was better in my day!'

And when it comes to art, works are also being generated by machines using AI. These machines 'learn' from analysing huge numbers of images. You can then put in some descriptive words, choose the style you like, and the AI will use what they have learned to create a new picture. *Voila* – art worthy of Vincent van Gogh-Bot.

Scientists themselves may be at risk of losing their jobs. Recently, a robot called Adam was able to design an experiment, carry it out and then interpret the results. Meanwhile, another robot called Eve working in Manchester University has been trying to identify anti-malarial drugs. Often these robots perform repetitive jobs. They might test millions of different drugs on experimental systems that are similar to diseases (like cells taken from patients), trying to find ones that work. They still need to be given a question and programmed to solve it, though, so there will still be a job for (at least) a few humans.

Medicine is already in the middle of a robotic revolution. Right now, robots can diagnose a disease and then prescribe the correct medicine, and even perform surgery. It's just a matter of working out what the disease is and then, from a huge amount of information, deciding on the best therapy. Medicine could become a long list of diseases on one side of the page and treatments on the other, with robotic doctors figuring it all out. Is that you, Dr Robotnik?!

But one profession where humans will most likely still be needed is nursing. A career like nursing is the perfect mixture of almost everything a machine finds difficult: fiddly motor skills (like putting a tube into an arm), specialist knowledge, and a wide variety of potential complications in the course of the job. And, obviously, the need to have empathy and put on a friendly face – something that robots haven't quite mastered!

It will be the doctors who become unwanted. Doctors are very expensive to train and hire, and they also make mistakes – they're only human, after all. The so-called Da Vinci robot can perform surgeries no human can because of its high precision. It can be remotely operated, meaning that a surgeon in one hospital can perform an operation in another.

Then there are robots like Mabu, a personal healthcare companion. Mabu will chat to a patient and pass the information on to doctors, giving the patient (and doctor) a situation where they don't have to talk to a human being if they don't want to, and still get treated. This would be great, especially if you wake up on the day of your appointment with terrible bed hair!

Apart from doctors, there are many aspects of healthcare where we will see more and more robots. The Japanese are especially interested in this, as they have an ageing population. Inventions there are making life easier for the elderly and their caregivers. A 'muscle suit' has been invented that gives the carer extra power when lifting a bed-bound patient. It looks like a backpack and takes off as much as 30 per cent of the strain of lifting someone. It is super expensive, though, and looks pretty silly, so I wouldn't recommend getting one for your heavy schoolbag just yet.

The Japanese have also developed a walking-stick-like device called the 'LIGHTBOT' that will guide visually impaired people to their destination, watching out for trip hazards along the way. It was developed because of a shortage of guide dogs in Japan, and the difficulties of keeping dogs as pets in a big city like Tokyo. It's not just people that robots will make unemployed – dogs need to watch themselves too! Job centres will soon be filled with sad, poor and lonely Labradors. No news on when there'll be a robot that will roll in poo and steal your dinner off your plate, which is probably a good thing for us.

Then there's the superhero we have all been waiting for. Yes! Is it a bird? Is it a plane? No, it's Robo-Nailist. This robot can't fly. It can't make itself invisible and it can't use X-ray vision, but it can ... wait for it ... paint your nails. Yes, Robo-Nailist has the power to paint your nails. I'm serious, that's it! However, it is a comfort to those who are too old or injured to paint their own nails. If your granny's hands  shake, then Robo-Nailist is here to save the day. It can coat those nails with a precision that no human can. Nailed it!

Journalism might also be in trouble. A firm called Narrative Science has a product called Quill. If you enter information structured in a certain way, it will produce a convincing and original news story. It is especially good at writing stories in sport and finance, where the information comes in a predictable format (like the number of goals scored or stock market prices). How do you know that what you are reading right now wasn't written by a robot … written by a robot … written by a …?

The saying goes that Google knows more about you than you do. Well, this could well be true. That little invention called 'cookies' is busy building a virtual you. In the old days, cookies were filled with chocolate, could be dipped in milk and were oh so good, but today they are forensic detectives. You see, when you go to a website, a small file called a cookie tracks what you do. Everything you have ever searched can be added together to see what you like and what you don't. The internet knows if you like knitting, eating Brussel sprouts and wearing your grandad's aftershave. It might then show you an ad for a sprout-scented aftershave in a woolly bottle. Gross!

RISE OF THE MACHINES

Is there any prospect of robots making us their slaves? There is evidence of robots cooperating with each other, and robots that act together without humans is a scary prospect. They could be comparing notes about who has the dirtiest kitchen. The robot revolution might have already begun: in Australia, a woman put a cleaning robot on the counter in her kitchen to clear up a cereal spill. She switched it off after the job was done. The robot, however, was clearly in despair with its life of hard work and had an existential crisis. It switched itself back on, went over to the hotplate, pushed over a coffee pot and then sat there until it burst into flames, destroying most of the apartment, and itself.

Then there's a thought experiment called the 'paperclip maximiser'. Think about it: a robot is programmed to make paperclips. It is so good at this job that it uses all the Earth's resources to achieve this goal. Then, it decides to get rid of humans, who are a drain on the system and might shut the robots down, stopping the production of paperclips. Eventually, this brilliant robot fills the entire universe up with paperclips. Gulp.

But how likely is this?

Many famous scientists and businesspeople have expressed their worries about an 'AI takeover' – a world in which we become the slaves of robots. Elon Musk, Bill Gates and the late, great Stephen Hawking have all gone on record to say they are worried that these clever machines could evolve and take charge. Hawking had some serious concerns about the rise of artificial intelligence in the future. The brilliant man was not predicting a doomsday scenario, but he was cautious. He said: 'It will either be the best thing that's ever happened to us, or it will be the worst thing. If we're not careful, it very well may be the last thing.'

Hawking could see the host of great opportunities for humans, but he was concerned about the possible speed of robotic evolution. Humans are limited by the slow pace of our ability to evolve. It takes us generations to redo, remake and upgrade – and even then we can't get rid of things like our granny's knobbly knees. Robots, however, can improve upon their own design much quicker. Or, as Hawking put it, 'Whereas the short-term impact of AI depends on who controls it, the long-term impact depends on whether it can be controlled at all.' Double gulp.

This may well sound like the stuff of sci-fi movies. Some people look at a world with 'good' and 'bad' robots – a kind of Optimus Prime versus Megatron situation. But evil in machines looks very, very unlikely. You see, as we build these machines, we have to build in checks and balances. We can't build a surgical robot that will make mistakes. Each piece of machinery and software must come with safety checks to ensure nothing goes wrong and no one gets hurt. This is particularly true of transport in the future. This is an area where robots will take over. Drones are already delivering parcels to homes, filming epic movies from the sky and carrying out undercover surveillance. I can imagine a street corner filled with angry and disappointed delivery drivers, film makers and spies. Never mind Steven Spielberg, you could be watching Steven Spiel-bot.

What is for sure is that we are looking at a future with driverless cars. Big companies such as Google are moving rapidly into a world where cars drive themselves. Lyon in France already has driverless buses, and Paris is planning for its inner city to be driverless as we speak. These vehicles will run on electricity and be charged by solar power. Car accidents, traffic jams and the need for parking spaces will be a thing of the past. Think of a world with city centres with no parking spaces. Paris' inner city has 150,000 parked cars. What could you do with all that free space? Create parks? Nature walks? Or a sanctuary for all those unemployed taxi drivers?

Better still, the morning commute or school run will be a breeze. You can sit in a car and have a caramel frappuccino, read your phone or do last night's maths before you get to school. Your granny can go to the bingo without any hassle, those with mobility issues can go wherever they like, and teenagers will no longer need the taxi of mum and dad. Without the need to drive, there will be a boom in racetracks where car lovers can go for a day – driving will be a hobby like golf or stamp-collecting!

On the downside, the Germans won't be happy. The German economy is propped up by car sales – it makes up one-third of the total. If they want to survive, they will need to team up with Google and become BM-Google-yous! But on the upside, it will be goodbye to petrol tax, speed tickets, parking fines and global emissions.

The reality is that technology and robots may not mean the end of the world, rather the start of a better, shinier, safer and cleaner one. The robotics industry currently employs almost a quarter of a million people as we speak, and it is exploding everywhere. We can look forward to a world full of robots helping us in so many ways: checking our health, painting our nails and driving us in a most leisurely way to anywhere we want to go. We will sit there in comfort, watching reruns of great Grand Prix races, reminding us of a bygone age when most people worked in difficult and boring jobs, often stuck for hours in traffic jams while polluting the Earth with fumes.

Roll on robots – we humans have nothing to lose but our chains.

CHAPTER 13

THE BEST
(AND WORST)
INVENTIONS
EVER BUILT

WE HUMANS HAVE invented some marvellous things. Think about trains, planes, submarines and space rockets that allow us to go where we want to go, faster than we ever have before. Even in our own homes we have smart speakers, laptops, iPhones and so on, which make our lives so convenient today. We have invented some ingenious things. Equally, it should be pointed out that we have also come up with some of the dumbest ideas ever. Thankfully, many never took off. Here's a few examples.

INVENTING OURSELVES

Project pigeon: Back in 1941, an American scientist called B.F. Skinner came up with what he thought was a lightbulb moment in the hope of defeating Adolf Hitler during World War II. Skinner's big idea to defeat the tyrant of the Western world? Erm, pigeons ... Sorry, yes! I said pigeons. Skinner proved that our little feathered friends could steer a missile towards a model ship by simply pecking at a target on a screen, which moved the rudders on the missile. Skinner's pigeons would continue to peck with incredible accuracy even in the last few seconds of rapid descent and with explosions going off all around them. Skinner's plan was to load three pigeons inside each missile cone and direct them to their eventual target. Sadly for Skinner, pigeon-driven bombs were cancelled just three years later in 1944. For some crazy reason, government officials felt they just couldn't trust pigeons to fly and control such dangerous weapons ... Hmm, I wonder why?

The escape coffin: Just in case a dead body decided it wasn't too keen on death anymore, in 1868 Franz Vester invented the escape coffin. This burial box came complete with an 'escape ladder' and a pull cord that would ring a bell in the local graveyard in which the body was buried. Vester thought people would be dying to get hold of it, but the escape coffin never really caught on ...

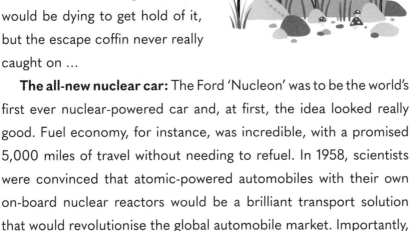

The all-new nuclear car: The Ford 'Nucleon' was to be the world's first ever nuclear-powered car and, at first, the idea looked really good. Fuel economy, for instance, was incredible, with a promised 5,000 miles of travel without needing to refuel. In 1958, scientists were convinced that atomic-powered automobiles with their own on-board nuclear reactors would be a brilliant transport solution that would revolutionise the global automobile market. Importantly, it was realised that even the smallest of car accidents could result in an entire city getting nuked and the brilliant plan, well, bombed!

Chlorofluorocarbons (CFCs): CFCs are nasty chemical compounds used in fridge units and aerosol cans that wreak havoc on the environment. CFCs combine with the ozone in our atmosphere and weaken the ozone layer. This important environmental barrier protects the Earth's surface from ultraviolet radiation from the sun. The thinning of the ozone layer over Antarctica came to be known as the ozone hole – like a hole in the roof of a greenhouse. In 1978, Sweden became the first country to ban CFC products. Later, the USA and Canada did the same. Now, CFC products are not allowed in most countries. But CFCs can stick around in the atmosphere for nearly a century, making this a very long-lived mistake. Our bad!

MAKING SPACE

In truth, you have to break a few eggs to make an omelette, and, despite mistakes, we have designed some of the most amazing machines you could ever imagine. One of these is the International Space Station (ISS). The ISS is the single most expensive item ever made, at a current estimated cost of $150 billion, which looks like this: $150,000,000,000. That's a lot of zeros!

The ISS is a 'liveable' working space station that is in low Earth orbit. This means it circles the Earth at a height between 330km and 435km above our heads. This piece of equipment is so big that you can see it with your naked eye as it scoots across the sky 15 or so times each day. It has human beings on it right now who are carrying out experiments in biology, chemistry, physics, astronomy and meteorology. It is regularly visited by Russian, American, European and Japanese vehicles. Astronauts or cosmonauts (as they're known in Russia) from 17 different countries have stayed up there and hopefully still send each other Christmas cards each year to remember the good old days in space.

But how on Earth (or off it) did we manage to get it up there in the first place? Well, it began in 1998, when the Russians launched parts of the ISS into space, which took more than 1,000 spacewalks. Then, it was gradually built in orbit using spacewalking astronauts and robotics. In 2000, the Russian spacecraft *Zvezda* launched and robotically added some true home comforts such as sleeping quarters, a toilet, a new kitchen, carbon dioxide scrubbers, which keep the air clean and breathable, as well as gym and communication equipment. Over the years, more and more bits were added to make the space station bigger and better. In 2010, 'the Cupola' was bolted on – this is basically an astronaut chill-out zone that gives those living up in space great views and a place to relax. Nice!

But how do humans survive up there in space? Well, the experts tell us that five basic things are needed: air, water, food, sanitation and suppression of heat. The air generated is exactly the same as we breathe here on Earth, with the same pressure as sea level. The carbon dioxide is removed by the scrubbers, as are human waste products like sweat and the smelly methane from the astronauts' bowels (delightful!). The station's electricity is generated by solar panels. Every piece of equipment generates heat, which is removed using ammonia that is then pumped through radiators outside the station.

The ISS is in constant contact with Earth, most notably with Mission Control in Houston (where hopefully they won't hear that most famous of space phrases: 'Houston, we have a problem'). They have advanced telecommunications networks, and even have Wi-Fi up there! (Better than your granny's house.)

A stint on the station usually lasts up to six months at a time. One cosmonaut holds the record for the human with the longest time in space: Sergei Krikalev spent a whopping 803 days, 9 hours and 39 minutes up there. Space tourists can also travel to the ISS, provided they pass the medical examination. Price per seat? Over $50 million. But get in line, as there is a waiting list! And people who go resent being called space tourists. They are often scientists and participate in experiments. Scientists are constantly testing things like how plants and human cells grow in zero gravity.

But what does an astronaut on the ISS do all day? Well, 6 a.m. is your astronaut wake-up call and space breakfast, which hopefully doesn't involve any aliens. At 8.10 a.m. the crew start work, which usually means a series of experiments, before an hour's lunch break at 1.05 p.m. The afternoon is the same as the morning and they turn in at 9.30 p.m., but it's not like an ordinary snooze. The windows are covered at night to help the astronauts sleep and stop them seeing the 16 sunrises and sunsets they would witness up there in a single day. The visitors, in spite of spending all that money, attach their sleeping bag to a space on the walls (Ryanair have denied any involvement in this). It is possible to sleep floating freely through the ISS, but this is generally avoided, in case the sleeping person bumps into equipment.

What about food? Deliveroo and Just Eat don't deliver to space for some strange reason, so all food is brought vacuum-packed in sealed bags. Taste is lower in zero gravity and so more spices are added. This is because fluids in the body get affected by the reduced gravity conditions, which messes with the astronauts' sense of smell. Fresh fruit and vegetables are occasionally delivered, which is a source of great excitement. The crew cook their own food. This means there are fewer arguments, and it gives them something to do. Any food that floats away must be caught, as it might clog up equipment. Remember *The Simpsons* episode where Homer smuggles a bag of crisps on-board? Dangerous stuff.

Hygiene is tricky. There used to be showers, but astronauts were only allowed to shower once a month, whether they needed it or not. Imagine the pong! This has been replaced with a water jet and wet wipes. The crew also have rinseless shampoo and edible toothpaste to save on water. There are two toilets, both designed by the Russians. Solid waste is stored for disposal, and urine is collected in anatomically correct funnels allowing men and women to pass urine. It is recycled into drinking water. As a result, astronauts in the ISS drink each other's pee. Yep! They recycle their urine and drink it ... Tasty.

One of the missions of the ISS is to prepare us for trips to the moon or to Mars. Human bodies are being tested in all kinds of ways in zero gravity, and a lot of space medicine is happening up there. Several things happen to us in zero gravity, including muscle-wasting, bone loss and fluids in our bodies behaving strangely. Astronauts have to make sure their muscles and bones keep working by exercising regularly.

The ISS also has an important educational role. Students on Earth can design experiments and can communicate with the astronauts via radio, videolink and email. The European Space Agency provides lots of free teaching material to use in classrooms. In May 2013, Commander Chris Hadfield played David Bowie's 'Space Oddity' on the ISS, and the film was released on YouTube. It has gotten over 51 million views, and is the first ever music video shot in space. It is also probably the most expensive video ever made!

SMASHING TIMES

The LHC or Large Hadron Collider looks like a bargain at €7.5 billion compared with the ISS, but it is still the largest and most expensive single machine ever built. The LHC is so big because it needs to be. It is made up of a tunnel that is 27km long and runs across the French-Swiss border.

This huge, expensive machine must surely be doing some important scientific work. Its job? To smash things together. 'Well, my little sister does that every day,' you might say, but the LHC smashes particles together, which are the building blocks that make up the entire universe. A bit different from smashing toy cars! When it is up and running, protons can get around the 27km tunnel in 90 millionths of a second. Then, they are smashed together at this incredible speed – that's where the word 'collider' in the name comes from – to break them down and see what they are made of. The scientists working at the LHC are trying to understand the fundamental questions in science, to understand why and how the universe works the way it does.

When it was first built, some scientists had a real fear that the LHC would be the beginning of the end for us humans. Some called it a 'Doomsday machine', while others said it was too powerful and could produce its own black hole and suck everything on Earth into it. Others theorised that it could produce dangerous particles that could get loose and turn everything on Earth into one hot, large lump of strange matter. This hasn't happened yet – we would probably notice – and the LHC has made many incredible discoveries that are helping us better understand the world.

The megamachines that are the ISS and the LHC are the culmination of the work of hundreds of thousands of people over many hundreds of years, building bit by bit on what has gone before. Both are propelled by the relentless and restless curiosity that drives the human race. When Neil Armstrong was the first human to walk on the moon, there were many, many people behind him whose work allowed him to make that small step. All that maths, science and engineering – all those teachers, all those exams – were worth it in the end.

All this exciting work on the ISS and the LHC is a brilliant example of what humans can achieve when they work together instead of fighting, bickering and pulling each other's underpants over each other's heads! And this is just the beginning. Who knows what these two machines will continue to tell us? And who knows what marvellous new machines will be built?

DID YOU KNOW?

The central part of the LHC is the world's largest fridge. It is set at a temperature colder than deep outer space, and the wires are so long that if you put each one after another they would stretch from the Earth to the sun and back six times with enough leftovers for about another 150 trips to the moon. That's a lot of cable ...

CHAPTER 14

WILL

WE STOP

ALL

DISEASES?

THE FACEBOOK FOUNDER Mark Zuckerberg has set up a foundation that aims to wipe out all diseases by 2100. An ambitious target, you might think, but we have come a very long way in our fight against disease in a fairly short time. Disease has always plagued us poor humans and is defined as a condition that harms the body's normal function, which usually has certain signs and symptoms. It basically stops us living our best life. Some of us get sick, and some of us don't. This can be because we carry variants of genes that make us sick. Or it can be because our lifestyle makes us sick. Or perhaps it's a combination of both, which is often the case. Some people get sick because of poverty, or just because of bad luck.

Medicine provides us with wonderful treatments for lots of the things that make us sick, but many diseases are still hard to treat. We all know about the huge effort going on to find new treatments and we often read about breakthroughs. But what does the future look like? Well, the signs are good. We now know more than ever about what goes wrong in the body when we become sick, in some cases right down to the tiny pieces inside that are causing mischief. The goal now is to stop these things going wrong or correct them when they do.

TINY TERRORS

Why are we so prone to nasty diseases in the first place? One idea is that once we stopped being nomadic, and began living closer together in villages and towns, infections were more likely to spread among us. And when we began living with our domesticated animals, their germs could spread to us (or vice versa), causing sickness. Thanks for the fleas, Rover ... you shouldn't have.

Two key players in the germ game are bacteria and viruses, but there are crucial differences between them. Bacteria are simply one large cell, but they can appear in a number of different guises. They can show up as throat, ear or skin infections, but they are also well trained at giving you things like food poisoning. These masters of disguise can come in all shapes and sizes: some are blobs, some are spirals and some look like little snakes.

Viruses, on the other hand, are around 20 times smaller than bacteria. These little burglars work by breaking into healthy cells and taking control of them. It's a bit like someone opening your car door at the traffic lights, pulling your family out and driving off. How dare they?! When these virus-filled cells spread, they make you very ill. This is how the cold, flu and the most recent nasty COVID-19 viruses work. They are always looking to hitch a ride on the next vehicle – or should I say, human. This is why you sneeze, cough and splutter when you have a cold. It's the virus saying, 'OK, take me to my next victim,' and – 'Achooo!' – the virus has landed.

The COVID-19 virus has been an expert at spreading itself around, which is why you are asked to wash your hands regularly, wear a mask and social distance. It is so contagious, it hopped all over the planet and went from epidemic to pandemic – the 'pan' bit means it crosses international borders. It is such a dangerous villain that governments had to put their countries into lockdowns, and we couldn't visit our friends or loved ones. Thankfully, though, our medical superheroes were on the job and came up with ways to fight back.

TREATMENTS OF YORE

The truth is that doctors and scientists have only really started to understand diseases in the fairly recent past. Previously, knowledge and beliefs could sometimes be questionable. The lack of understanding of the body made for some strange practices.

In ancient Egypt, if you had a toothache, then your local doctor would tell you to eat some poo. If you had a cut leg, then you would be advised to rub some poo on it. In ancient Rome, they used mouthwash to clean their teeth, but instead of gargling something like 'Minty Fresh Pine Breeze' they used urine. Yep, they gargled wee. It probably had an ad campaign that said, 'A slosh of pee is nicer than a good cup of tea'. Think things can't get any worse? Well, let me take you across to ancient Greece, where clever doctors would work out what was wrong with you by looking at your puke. In fact, they didn't just look at it or poke it with a big stick. They would eat it. Lovely.

One favourite of doctors back in the day was to place leeches on problem areas like an infected arm or use them to treat a heart condition. Imagine you have an infected toe, and the doctor whips out a mini version of the Star Wars alien Jabba the Hutt. Basically, a slimy slug-like creature with an enormous mouth filled with around 300 teeth that simply loves to suck your blood. Leeches are rarely used in medicine nowadays, which is no bad thing, as they caused the deaths of lots of people. That said, they have made a bit of a comeback in medicine, to help regulate blood flow around an area of surgery. You see, these little beauties can drink 10 times their body weight in blood in one sitting. That's like you sitting at lunchtime and trying to eat about 500 large pizzas ... Don't even think about it!

Wriggly maggots were also a bit of a household favourite. Yes, if you suffered with dead or infected tissue on your skin, then doctors would pop some maggots on the area. These lovelies would throw up on the wound as their puke is filled with special chemicals that break up the flesh. Then, they would gobble it all back up again.

And in 1796, a scientist tried scraping pus off one patient and injecting it into another ... but that treatment actually worked! A guy called Edward Jenner (no relation to Kris Jenner) gets the credit. He noticed that milkmaids rarely got a horrible viral disease called smallpox. He figured out (or more likely was told by a farmer neighbour) that this was because they already had the milder disease of cowpox. This led Jenner to test cowpox on a young boy called James Phipps. This was the scientific method in action: come up with a hypothesis (in this case, that cowpox could protect against smallpox), then test it. He scraped the pus from cowpox blisters on the hands of a milkmaid who had caught cowpox from a cow called Blossom. He injected it into James Phipps, then tried to infect him with smallpox and – hey presto – he was protected from smallpox! (And what thanks did Blossom get? Well, her hide now hangs on the wall of the St George's Medical School library ...)

What had happened was that the boy's immune system had reacted to cowpox, but it had caused only a mild disease. Cowpox and smallpox viruses are very alike, so when the boy was given smallpox, his immune system had been trained to recognise smallpox, and dealt with it easily. Once that was understood, we were away, and vaccination against smallpox began to take off. Amazingly, this virus was wiped out completely in 1980!

Vaccination works something like a war, where the first encounter with the enemy is a bunch of old guys who are easily beaten. Then when the younger, fitter troops arrive in the same uniform they are recognised quickly and eliminated. Following on from Jenner, many other vaccines were developed. We now have vaccines for many diseases, including our new arrival, COVID-19.

Antibiotics, on the other hand, kill bacteria on contact. Penicillin was the first of these to be discovered, through another fairly

WILL WE STOP ALL DISEASES? 163

disgusting process. One day, a scientist called Alexander Fleming noticed that a mould growing on a dish filled with bacteria had killed all of the bacteria. The mould had actually come from a lab below him that was run by an Irish doctor called Charles La Touche. La Touche had been collecting cobwebs in the East End of London to explore if they caused asthma attacks. The cobwebs had captured the fungus *penicillium*, which makes penicillin to protect itself from bacteria. It was this that somehow blew out of La Touche's lab and into Fleming's, killing the bacteria. Lucky for us his windows were open! Fleming called this lovely stuff 'mould juice', and it was the first ever antibiotic.

Now, these clever drugs save millions of lives every year. The big breakthroughs have limited the devastating effects of viruses and changed the game in our favour. But be warned, overuse can make some bacteria immune to this medical superhero, so we need to use them carefully.

A SICK FUTURE?

We are now in a new era, where so-called diseases of wealth are killing a lot of humans. In other words, we now have enough money to eat and drink ourselves to death! It's a bit like the earlier mentioned maggots who can eat 10 times their own weight at one sitting. Well, feed them only fat-filled red meat and sugary drinks and see what happens ... This is why a healthy lifestyle is so important – your PE teacher was right all along.

HELLO, MY NAME IS

Billy

In addition, we are living longer than we have ever done before. The poor Victorians were lucky to make it to 40, but the average person born in Ireland today can expect to live to the ripe old age of 93. But with that comes new challenges. Being old looks like a disease: our eyes and ears don't work well, we have aches and pains, and we mightn't be able to lead as full a life as we used to. Inflammation sets in, which means that our immune systems begin to attack our own bodies. We can treat this with some medicines. Our ancient ancestors noticed that certain plants could help inflammation, like willow bark. Now, we can take the useful parts of these plants and use them to make drugs like aspirin artificially in labs.

As we live longer, diseases that affect our brains take hold. Our memories are truly amazing – our brains are like an enormous hard drive storing millions and millions of memories. You can't remember everything you've ever done, but you will retain the important stuff like your name, address and that one time you bathed in cold beans (maybe you should erase that memory?). The part of the brain where all these memories are stored is called the hippocampus, but as we age the hippocampus gets smaller, which explains why your dad might search the house for car keys or walk into a room and say, 'Now what did I come in here for?'

The good news is that there is great research in this area and new breakthroughs are happening as we speak. Very soon, we could have a situation where the main diseases that affect us are prevented, slowed or cured. What might we die of then? Total and utter boredom on a landmark birthday like your 251st?

Other exciting developments include the fixing of broken DNA in mutated genes. Remember CRISPR? Research shows that CRISPR can be used to cure heart disease even before you are born by correcting the faulty gene in the fertilised egg. You're basically fixed before you knew you needed to be.

Stem cells are another exciting option. The fertilised egg contains these special cells which have all the information to make all the organs in your body. As you develop, the cells branch off

and become specialists in, say, making skin or liver cells. Scientists have been able to wind the tape back to those original stem cells, which could then grow into whatever your body needs. Some companies are even taking stem cells from your bones, storing them away for the future and then hopefully using them later to build a new you. Some scientists think it will be a bit like replacing parts in an old car, or a human being drivethrough. Imagine ordering a new version of yourself? 'I'd like a new knee because this one is dodgy. Oh! And can I get fries with that?'

Other areas of progress are starting to look more like science fiction and the movies than scientific fact. Dr Bertalan Meskó describes himself as a 'Medical Futurist' and has written a paper called 'A guide to the future of medicine'. He says that powered exoskeletons as seen in movies like *Avatar* and *The Avengers* already exist. This technology means people who are paralysed and can no longer use their legs can get up and walk around. They can take a walk down to the shops or simply walk their dog. He predicts a future that has digestible digital devices. In other words, you get up each morning, have breakfast and swallow a 'smart pill' that will then monitor your temperature, pulse and blood pressure from inside your body – cool, eh? Even cooler, he thinks the medical world and the gaming world will collide in what he calls 'gamified-based wellbeing'. This means young and old will get on their gaming console and complete activities that make them fitter, faster, stronger and smarter.

Better still, he sees a time when every household owns a humanoid robot – a robot that looks like a human. (I know, don't get the one that looks like your man in town with the pointy head.) These cool contraptions will be carers for the sick, companions for the lonely and the elderly, and help children with things like autism to understand the world better.

What is certain is that the best way to prevent disease is with the age-old approach of having a good diet, good exercise and good sleep patterns. Perhaps we should all follow the advice of Jonathan Swift in *Gulliver's Travels* when he wrote the line: 'The best three doctors are: Doctor Diet, Doctor Quiet and Doctor Merryman.' In other words, eat well, sleep well and laugh well. After all, laughter is the best medicine, so keep on smiling!

CHAPTER 15

NO NEED
TO WORRY
ABOUT
GROWING
OLD

THE ROCK BAND Oasis had a hit song called 'Live Forever'. This is wishful thinking – at the moment this idea is a bridge too far. We all grow old. Almost all life on Earth grows old and dies. Things like bacteria and yeast are single-celled and just keep dividing and dividing. A tiny jellyfish named *Turritopsis dohrnii* seems to be able to live forever – it can return to its earliest stage of life as it ages or gets sick. But for us humans, our cells keep dividing and then, one day, stop.

Most of us die of diseases, and, as we saw in the previous chapter, many of us die of diseases of ageing. Our bodies eventually pack it in, and perhaps an infection that we would normally fight kills us, or our hearts or brains eventually run down. Apart from accidental death or a disease like cancer, our bodies will naturally age and die. This can be a bit of a bummer for some people ... but not us, for we are scientists! Let's have a look.

LONG LIVES

Luckily, today, we can live for a very, very long time. Most people will reach 80 years, some will get to 90 and some even further. The longest a human being has ever lived (that we know of) is Jeanne Calment of France (1875–1997), who lived to the age of 122 years, 164 days. We don't quite know how she managed this! She herself said: 'Always keep a smile. I attribute my long life to that. I believe I will die laughing. That's part of my program.'

Jeanne Calment's age is likely to be close to the absolute limit for humans. There are limits on all living things. The average lifespan for mice is three years. For cats, it is 12 years and for dogs it is 13. What sets these limits, we are not fully sure. We used to think it was to do with size – the bigger you are, the longer you live. But one creature called a Hydra – a teeny freshwater creature with tentacles – can live for ... wait for it ... 1,400 years. Imagine its 1,300th birthday party ... 'Yehhhhh! Just another hundred to go!'

Top of the human long-life-league table is Japan. The Japanese are the oldest nation on Earth. Ireland isn't too bad, coming in at 19th. Where you are born in some ways decides how long or short your life might be. Sierra Leone in Africa has a life expectancy of just 50.1 years. Sadly, this is due to poverty and widespread diseases like AIDS that have ravaged the country and caused people to die much sooner than they should.

But overall, we are undoubtedly living longer and will continue to do so. We are, as some scientists say, 'Turning Japanese'. In 1950, 5 per cent of the Japanese population was over 65. It is now 50 per cent. This is probably due to a high fish diet and few sugary drinks. But there is a downside. The Japanese are ageing and they are not having enough children. As a result, they are the first country to sell more adult diapers than those for babies (sorry if you're eating at the moment). Playgrounds are being converted into exercise areas for the elderly. Make room on the roundabout for Grandad!

One key factor in living longer seems to be our diet. In studies of people who lived to 100 years or more, the general findings showed that these people ate smaller meals and did not carry extra weight. Other studies show that if you exercise in your fifties, you can add 2.5 years to your life (I don't know how they did the sums on this one!). Strange factors can add and take away years. Believe it or not, marriage gives you plus seven years. Marriage is especially helpful for men. It is thought routine, less stress and a better lifestyle makes you live longer. Divorce, on the other hand, is minus years and shortens life. Again, stress can be a factor.

What decides how long a creature lives might come down to heartbeats. On average, humans have 2.21 billion heartbeats in their lifetime. It also might mean that if you exercise and increase your number of heartbeats per minute, it might actually shorten your life – which gives me the perfect excuse to avoid exercise. Just joking – exercise is shown to help us live longer too (but not too vigorous exercise, as it can damage the tissues and reverse the effects. So slow down!).

Vampires like Dracula have long been portrayed as immortal in books, comics and movies. Their secret was going out at night and drinking new blood, but the truth may not be that far away. In a series of, let's say, 'strange' experiments, scientists took old mice and transfused them with young mouse blood. The results were amazing. The old mice became healthier, had better joints and could see better. This could be the end of the song 'Three Blind Mice' entirely ...

WORM FOOD

Studies in the animal kingdom support the link between food and long life. This is especially true of one microscopic worm called a nematode. These tiny creatures live on rotting mushrooms but the people who study ageing love them ... I know, first-class weirdos or what? These worms live only for a few weeks, which means it's easy to see if their life has been long or short. Also, unlike us humans who have billions of cells, the nematodes have exactly 1,096 cells in total and that means there are few enough cells to count, trace and study.

Back when I worked in Cambridge University, I met a scientist called John Sulston and I asked him what he was working on. He told me that he spent eight hours a day, every day, looking down a microscope counting worm cells and following them! (I know – nice guy, though.) John had the last laugh because in 2002, he went on to win the Nobel Prize for his ground-breaking work, which showed exactly how cells live and die. When scientists improved the nutrition in the nematodes, they extended their lives by twice as much. If we translate that into humans, we could very comfortably live to 200 years or more.

So, can we live longer if we watch what we eat? The science all points that way. The Mediterranean diet seems perfect, as it is full of fruit, olive oil, seafood and vegetables. The villagers of a little remote Italian town called Acciaroli are the perfect case study. In Acciaroli, more than 300 people have lived to be over 100 years old. As a result, scientists from all over the world have now descended on poor Acciaroli to torment the over-100s by chasing them up alleyways, making them open their mouths to say 'ahhhh', hitting their knees with little hammers to see how they react and taking their poo to labs to inspect it. (By the way, about one-quarter of your poo is alive! Don't worry, it won't take off and chase you up the road like a scientist looking for a 100-year-old Italian, it's just live bacteria.) The scientists are, of course, trying to find what keeps these people going. The diet is a big part of it, and the village is on a hilltop, which means they walk more than most on average. So, should we all wander around eating seafood pizza all day? Sounds like a great idea.

THE BEST YEARS

Will all this research be worthwhile? If we do find drugs to help us with ageing, it's unlikely that they will let us live beyond a certain span, which is probably around 120 years, unless we come up with

ways to keep replacing our worn-out parts as we age. Instead, we'll just slow down the problems of ageing.

But maybe ageing isn't all bad. One thing that a series of studies has shown is that we peak at different things at different ages. When you look back on your life, will you say that you loved being 12 or 47 or maybe 75? Scientists have been studying a wide range of both physical and mental skills to figure out at what age we peak for each of them. There have been some very interesting results. You are best able to learn a second language when you are seven or eight years of age. That seems to be when the mind is at its most receptive, probably because it's when we listen to the advice of our parents (well … sometimes). Try to learn a second language past 30 and it's much more difficult. So, start on the books now – *hola, guten tag, nîn hâo, asalama alaikum, konnichiwa!*

Your brain-processing power, on the other hand (your ability to understand information and remember long strings of numbers), peaks at 18. This is good for when you are in third level education. Your ability to remember unfamiliar names peaks at 22. This is possibly because you are now out in the wild, and you don't want to go offending the chief of another tribe by forgetting his name. Your status anxiety is at its peak too, which probably explains some of the terrible fashion trends around.

Your muscle strength will peak at age 25. You will run your best marathon at age 28. And your bone mass will peak at age 30, because that is when you can retain the most calcium in your bones. If you are a chess player, you will peak at age 31!

According to a study of 10,000 people (which is a very large number and therefore probably gave correct results), your ability to understand someone else's emotional state peaks in your forties and fifties. And then it gets better as you get older for certain things – your ability in maths peaks at age 50, your vocabulary in your late sixties. You feel much more comfortable in your own body in your seventies and, finally, and we all know this, you are at your wisest when you are over 70. So, it really is true that wisdom comes with age.

One striking result from several studies is that life satisfaction peaks at two ages: 23 and 69. This is the case whether you have children or whether you are single or maybe even whether you support the Irish football team. It seems to be built into us for some unknown reason. Crucially, after 70 we rate our lives as being at least a seven out of ten. When we're younger, we rate it lower.

As a wise old man once said: 'At age twenty we worry about what others think of us. At age forty we don't care what they think of us. And at age sixty we discover they haven't been thinking of us at all.' So, it's well worth hanging on in there and ageing gracefully (and hopefully healthily), as things will only get better.

CHAPTER 16

DON'T
FEAR
THE
REAPER

THIS ONE WON'T make you laugh, but it needs to be said – you are going to die. I know, it's not the cheeriest of thoughts, but you should by now know that for us scientists no topic is off the table. We want to and need to get right in there, right up to our elbows. Death is an undeniable truth. Think about it, why are there so many undertakers around? Eh?!

However, it's not all doom and gloom. On a very positive note, a child born in Ireland today can expect to live to the ripe old age of 100 – that has never happened before and again it's down to science. Better medicines, new technologies and better lifestyles all come together to make us live longer than we ever could before.

DEAD SURE

One thing about death that has worried people for hundreds of years is how we actually know that someone is dead. It may seem obvious now, but in the past it wasn't (unless, of course, someone had their head chopped off). Say you lived a few hundred years ago and old Grandpa (who back then was probably 40 years of age) seemed to have croaked. You didn't call for a doctor, you called for the priest, who would make the determination of death. All the priest would have at his (never her!) disposal would be outward signs of death. They might hold a mirror over Grandpa's mouth to see if it

 clouded over. Or stick a feather under his nose to see if it moved. In the 1700s, enough was known about the human body to check for his heartbeat, but the stethoscope wasn't invented until 1816. There was still some gruesome science along the way. Take Balfour's Test, for example. This 'test' required long thin needles with flags on the end – yes, flags – to be stuck into the heart. If the flags 'waved,' the heart was still beating, and then the person was deemed to be still alive!

However, doctors began to realise that although outwardly the person appeared to be dead (with no detectable heartbeat or breathing), they might in fact be still alive and perhaps might recover. This phenomenon led to people being buried alive, which wasn't especially unusual in the nineteenth century. Remember the coffin bell from Chapter 13? Doesn't seem like such a silly invention now!

Today there are all kinds of ways to attempt to resuscitate someone, or keep them alive. A person can be hooked up to a ventilator and other machines to keep their heart beating. But in the 1950s, doctors recognised that people were being kept 'alive' by machines. They weren't coming back, because of brain damage that couldn't be repaired. We therefore now define death as being 'brain dead'. A person who meets this definition of death has lost the ability to breathe on their own. Breathing is essential to get the oxygen your body needs to keep the lights on. Simply put, dying starts when the body doesn't get enough oxygen to survive.

RISKY BUSINESS

In movies and TV, death tends to be fairly dramatic. The real truth is that most people die gradually, just like an old machine whose parts have worn out. There won't be death by asteroid, no high-speed car chases or exploding space rockets. No, the scientists have crunched the numbers on this and to be honest it will all be rather ordinary. So ordinary, in fact, that the scientists have made a risk scale for it. Yep! The science nerds have basically made a 'How to Die' scale and it tries to measure the risk of death for a person doing a certain thing. The Duckworth Scale, to give it its proper name, is named after its inventor, Dr Frank Duckworth. The scale runs from 0 to 8, with 0 being the safest kind of activity you could be involved in and 8 being one that will result in certain death.

Dr Duckworth has graded a whole range of human activities from washing up to flying on a plane, and you might just be surprised at some of the results. For example, if you are a 35-year-old male who smokes 40 cigarettes a day, then you will be very high on the scale with a score of 7.1 – a score which is, amazingly, almost as dangerous as playing Russian roulette with a single bullet loaded in a gun!

What's interesting is the boring reality of this research. A single car journey with your dad is more life-threatening than an asteroid. And a bit of vacuuming and washing up is more likely to get a person than murder. (Thankfully, but watch those dishes!)

LEVEL ON SCALE	HUMAN ACTIVITY
0.0	Complete safety (living on Earth unharmed for a year)
0.3	A single 160km rail journey
1.6	Being hit by an asteroid (in the lifetime of a newborn male)
1.7	A single 160km aeroplane flight
1.9	A single 160km car journey (driven by your dad)
4.2	Rock climbing (only once)
4.6	Murder (in the lifetime of a newborn male)
5.5	Vacuuming; washing up; walking down the street; car accident (in the lifetime of a newborn male); accidental fall (newborn male)
6.3	Rock climbing (for over 20 years)
6.4	Deep-sea fishing (for over 40 years)
7.1	Smoking (35-year-old male, 40 a day)
7.2	Russian roulette (single game, one bullet)
8.0	Russian roulette (single game, six bullets); jumping off the Eiffel Tower; lying down in front of a speeding train

BODY BREAKDOWN

It seems, though, that once you pop your clogs then that's it. Well, again, it's not straightforward. The point of no return appears to be what the scientists call 'biological death' – this is when the heart has stopped beating and the brain cells start to die due to a lack of oxygen and resuscitation is impossible, but even then, old death has one last trick to play. The 'Lazarus sign' is a weird and disturbing trick of the body but is thankfully a rare occurrence. A spinal reflex in the newly deceased can produce a scene that you might expect in a horror movie. You see, the neurons in the spinal cord are not yet dead and cause a reflex, making the person's arms rise up and cross over across the chest before falling back down – an event sure to make a few people jump!

One thing we don't know is what exactly a dying person is feeling. However, some people have come back from death's door and reported a feeling of peace and wellbeing. These are called near-death experiences (or NDEs in the trade), and people's experiences are strangely similar. Some report an out-of-body experience, a feeling of floating above their own body. Some report seeing a bright light and moving towards it. Some even say they see dead relatives beckoning them. These things are remarkably common across all cultures.

Once a person passes, then a whole new area of science kicks in. This is called 'forensic science' – a field often highlighted in movies and crime shows where really good-looking scientists with cool suntans and blindingly white teeth turn up at the scene of a crime to study the dead body to work out how and when the person died.

Estimating the time of death is tricky. One method scientists use to try to pinpoint the exact time of death is a machine called LABRADOR, which stands for the easy to remember Lightweight Analyser for Buried Remains and Decomposition Odour Recognition. This device 'sniffs' out the odours released by chemicals in the body as it decomposes. A death sniffer ... who knew?

After death, the body starts to break down or decompose. With the energy gone, the decay process starts, and this is where it gets interesting ... Where the body is will dictate the rate of decay. For example, if the body is refrigerated, decay will be slowed. If placed in a lead-lined coffin, it can take decades to completely decompose, but if left outside or buried in soil, it will take only a few months for a body to disappear.

The crime scene scientists are mega smart and know there is a simple timeline of events once a person has died. They know that within minutes, carbon dioxide starts to build up in the body. Remember, when they were alive, a person would breathe this toxic stuff out, just like an exhaust removing the toxic gases from a car. This carbon dioxide in the body causes cells to burst open and the tissues in the body start to get chewed up from within. Then, after about 30 minutes, the blood starts to pool at the lowest point and, disturbingly, turns a person's underside black. Then the calcium in the bones leaks out and causes the body to stiffen up. This is called 'rigor mortis' and is the science behind some of the old sayings you may have heard like 'she's as stiff as a board'.

If you're still reading this, you might think the idea of a career in forensic science might just be for you. Now your stomach is going to be really tested. After all the gases, bursting cells, blackening and stiffening bodies come the bacteria, followed by a whole host of creepy-crawlies. The first creatures to arrive are flies, including the common housefly. There is a system at work here. You see, all the flies don't just pile into the body willy-nilly – different species of flies arrive at different times, and this gives the forensic scientist lots of valuable clues. In fact, if you really like the insect part of death, then you could actually specialise as a forensic entomologist. They study bodies to see which insects arrive when and which maggots grow first (maggots grow from flies' eggs that have been laid on the body). Beetles tend to arrive later to the party, as they prefer a body that has decomposed for longer – picky eaters, I guess. Speaking of, hope you're not having lunch at the moment.

Eventually, depending on climate, after a few months or years all that is left is bone. No creature on Earth can digest bone and, often the bones will crumble, turn to dust and get blown away. This is where the saying 'ashes to ashes, dust to dust' comes from. Now, we have a fully recycled person.

Death is a natural process that all bodies go through at some stage. As scientists, understanding this process can help us understand ourselves and what happens to our loved ones once they pass away. What you think has happened to the essence of the person who has died will depend on your religious or cultural beliefs. Some people are comforted by the notion of seeing that person again in some kind of afterlife. We don't really know for sure what happens. But what we do know for sure is that our physical bodies will break down into the same building blocks that make up the rest of the universe – the soil, the trees and even the stars.

DID YOU KNOW?

Back in 1752, medical schools had already started using dead bodies to learn more about medicine. The UK government passed a law that allowed the bodies of those who had been executed for murder to be used in the medical schools. Sadly, there weren't enough murderers to go around, and the schools started offering money to anyone who had a spare dead body lying about.

A new career emerged, which had the job title of grave robber or bodysnatcher. Your job meant you hung about graveyards and dug up fresh dead bodies. The older, decomposed ones were no good. The schools would pay you about

€8 for a body in good condition ... I know, hardly enough to get a McWhopper meal, but in today's money that would be about €1,200. (Ah! You're listening now, aren't you?) The bodysnatching trend saw people bury their relatives in coffins with padlocks on or in iron coffins. Weird or what?

CHAPTER 17

HOW

TO

DEFY

DEATH

S O, YOU DON'T like the sound of all that death stuff too much. Would you prefer to live forever? If you would, then you simply pay loads of money to a company that will freeze your body and place you in a big fridgey thing. You leave instructions that when the world of science finds a cure for the disease that killed you, you are to be thawed out, placed in your best-looking outfit and sent out to meet what will probably, by then, be your great-great-great-grandchildren. (Not weird at all, eh?)

BODY FREEZE

Seriously, though, this field of science is big, big business. It is known as 'cryonics' – the science of freezing you like a fish finger, thawing you out later and jumpstarting you before letting you loose on the world once more. The name comes from the Greek word *kryos* meaning 'cold', and we're talking super cold – you'd be frozen to a temperature of −196 °C. That's colder than cold. To get you that cold, you'd need to float in a tank of liquid nitrogen. Which is exactly what you're paying for!

Freezing needs to be carried out as soon as possible after death to limit the damaging effects that happen following death. The next step is to drain the body of all its fluids, and to replace those fluids with an anti-freeze that stops ice crystals from forming when the deep freeze begins. This is important because ice crystals can damage the delicate structures in the body, like the many tiny blood vessels that course through us.

The body is then packed in ice and transported to a cryonic facility, either in the USA or Russia, depending on who you're paying. Once it arrives, the body is put in a special arctic sleeping bag and then cooled to −110 °C over several hours using nitrogen gas. This is a very low temperature. Over the course of the next two weeks, the body is progressively cooled even further, down to −196 °C. Very, very cold indeed. Then the spooky thing happens. The body is suspended in a big vat of liquid nitrogen, bobbing away like a cork. It is transferred to the 'patient care bay', where it will be kept until either the money runs out or the technology is found to bring the body back to life in full health, emerging like Lazarus from the tomb.

The medical community isn't totally on-board with cryonics. This is because it is currently not reversible, and it's not known whether it ever will be. But it is a very active area of science, with several laboratories experimenting with the freezing of various animals and, more importantly, organs for transplantation. If it were possible to freeze, say, a kidney for use in a surgery, this might increase the chances of the transplantation working. Often, transplanted organs are rejected because they have been kept too long outside the body. They effectively go off!

The first person ever to be cryopreserved was Dr James Bedford in 1967. Since then, it is estimated that around 250 people have been cryopreserved in the USA, with another 1,500 having requested it in their will. There has been a strong rumour that Walt Disney's head is frozen in a cryonics facility in the USA, although this has been hotly denied. Elsa from *Frozen* won't be out of a job anytime soon!

A related but slightly different field is cryopreservation. Here they don't freeze all of you but a bit of a leg or a brain or a kidney. 'What use is that?' I hear you shout. 'I can't walk around as a kidney in three hundred years' time!'

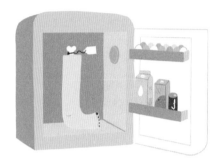

But studies are showing lots of positive results. One company claims to have frozen a rabbit kidney to a chilly −135 °C Celsius and then brought it back for a successful transplant. Another company in California claims to have frozen a rabbit's brain and then recovered it to a 'near perfect' state (whatever that means ... poor bunnies – gives a whole new meaning to 'brain freeze').

Other companies are looking at the idea of taking some of your body's cells, storing them and as you grow older and things start to wear out, they grow you something new like a new kidney or heart and simply replace it. This is an amazing idea, because your body won't reject the new kidney or heart because they are 'you'. Your body will welcome the new addition because it won't be 'foreign' like the current donor situation. You'd be you, except a different you. Make sense?!

The brain might be tricky, as brain transplants have yet to be mastered, and may never be. But other scientists are speculating that it might one day be possible to upload the information in your brain into a supercomputer and that might then take charge, running all those fresh organs that are grown in the lab. Or perhaps

operate an avatar. This seems like science fiction, right? A world where when we age, we simply replace old organs with new ones and hook our bodies up to a supercomputer ...

LIFE AT THE EXTREMES

Human life has always been seen as delicate. We don't like it too hot or too cold. We like it, as Goldilocks says, 'just right'. From a planetary perspective, Earth has it just right for life to thrive. But even on this brilliant blue ball, we don't like things too extreme. If we travel to warmer climates, we usually need help in the form of air conditioning, a nice pool or an ice-cold ice cream. If we venture to colder places, we wear warm, heavy clothing, usually stay indoors and opt for a nice fire. Recently, though, studies have looked at the extreme conditions under which life can survive.

The planet has ingenious microorganisms that not only thrive in such a range of challenges, but can also survive the harsh conditions of outer space, an environment with extreme radiation, vacuum pressure, changing temperatures and low gravity. These practically indestructible little creatures are called extremophiles because they can live in the most extreme conditions we could possibly imagine. They offer hope that if they can endure these elements, then maybe one day we could too.

Maybe the strangest of all extremophiles is a tiny, yet mighty, creature called a tardigrade or, to use their cuter name, 'water bear'. These are remarkable little creatures who measure just 1.5mm in length, but they appear to be the toughest of the tough. They can survive in some of the most extreme conditions, including −272 °C (which is close to absolute zero), plus 150 °C, gamma rays that would zap other organisms, and can easily cope with pressures as high as 5,000 atmospheres – which is the same pressure felt at Planet Earth's deepest trenches. These guys have even survived and made it back from the extremes of outer space without damage (and you thought superheroes and Bear Grylls were tough?!).

And it's not just extremophiles who can do incredible things. There is a range of clever creatures who are able to 'die' and then come back to life. These guys are so cool that if there were a TV talent show for freezing yourself and bringing yourself back to life, then these creatures would be the stars of that show. Let's give it the catchy name of 'Dying On Ice' – I think that name will catch on. Anyway, these two would be the winners, out in front of all the other contestants. The wood frog known as *Rana sylvatica* freezes in the winter with 45 per cent of its body turning to ice. Incredibly, this tough little guy stops breathing, its heart stops beating and blood flow ceases. It makes special proteins that preserve its organs during

this time. As a result, this animal can 'die' for 11 days at −4 °C, bring itself 'back to life' and then hop off. The other star is the Arctic ground squirrel. It is especially skilled as it is a warm-blooded mammal that can survive temperatures as low as −2.9 °C for 20 days or more. Take a bow, Frog 'n' Squirrel!

AN IMMORTAL FUTURE?

Will we ever crack the code for immortality? At this stage we don't know, but it's fun to think about and perhaps write a script for a Hollywood movie. All this research into defying death is fascinating, and the scientists involved have discovered some amazingly brilliant things. But we also need to ask some questions about what they mean:

- 'Do you want to live forever?'
- 'Would you get bored after a while?'
- 'Would a completely rebuilt you be the same you?'
- 'Would you have the same personality or be someone completely different?'
- 'Will only rich people be able to pay for these medical advances or will everyone have a fair chance?'

These are all important questions that come alongside brilliant medical developments. And we have to think about them carefully before we get ahead of ourselves. Because the truth is that we are getting smarter and smarter and better and better at the science behind what makes us work. And that has to be the coolest thing ever. Except for those bodies bobbing around in the cryogenic tanks, of course. Brrr.

CHAPTER 18

WILL

WE

BECOME

EXTINCT?

WE HUMANS ARE very clever but, amazingly, we are also very dumb. We have managed to conquer this planet. We can boast that we have gone to the highest mountain and the deepest sea trench (which, believe it or not, is a greater distance than going to the highest mountain!). We have left the planet and gone to the moon. So, we know we can do amazing stuff, but equally we can wreck the shop when we want to. Who killed the dodo? Yes, it was us dodos. Who tried to kill us all in World Wars I and II? Yes, us again. Who is currently making the planet heat to boiling point? Well, I think you can guess.

We might think of ourselves as a super species – a group of people who are simply invincible – but nothing could be further from the truth. Life on Earth is actually a very fragile thing. At least five times in Earth's history it nearly became extinct – ice ages, meteor strikes and gamma ray bursts from a distant star – but we have somehow managed to dodge the bullet each time.

Scientists, being big smarty-pants have, of course, got sophisticated names for these events. Yes, when they all meet up they can't even just call them meetings. No, 'meetings' isn't fancy enough. Wait for this – they must be conferences, convocations, colloquies, forums, confabulations or symposiums and all their sandwiches are cut into triangles and are filled with things like watercress and cucumber!

Anyway, in science-speak, the end of the world has a few specific references that the scientists get very giddy about such as 'mass extinctions', 'extinction events' or 'biotic crisis'. 'Biotic' means living, so a biotic crisis means – well, you know what it means for us ... Gulp!

EXTINCTION EVENTS

Seriously, though, how have we nearly popped our clogs all these times? First up was what the brainiacs called the GOE – the Great Oxygenation Event – and it happened 2.5 billion years ago. There was a really simple change on Earth where too much oxygen built up. That might seem ridiculous, as oxygen helps us to do stuff like breathe and all, but oxygen is actually very toxic stuff.

So, how did all this oxygen build up? Well, that's the genius part. Bacteria called Cyanobacteria started to evolve and they learned the cleverest trick of all – how to make their own food. That seems incredibly simple to us now. After all, how hard is it to make a ham-sam? Or pop a Mars bar in your gob? But before all our technology, before there were even cocoa beans, these bacteria flicked the switch that made us all exist. They took carbon dioxide from the air and used the sun's energy. Then they combined it with water and made more of themselves. They had made that wonderful stuff we all need to live – carbohydrates or, more simply, sugars. This might sound very underwhelming, but this was the start of photosynthesis – the process where plants can turn the sun's energy into food.

Back 2.5 billion years ago, the Cyanobacteria kept busily working away and making more and more oxygen until the Earth's atmosphere was filled with the stuff. Scientists know this happened by looking at rocks from the time. The clever Cyanobacteria evolved protective measures to ward off the toxic oxygen levels, but other organisms were not so well equipped and died out in huge numbers. For the lucky ones, life took off at a rapid pace – it was a bit like being at a party when someone cranks the music up really loud. Lots of people leave, but those with headphones on carry on dancing and go on to make more headphone-wearing babies. In this case, the loud music was oxygen, and only those who liked it stayed. Strangely, the GOE – the almost complete destruction of life on Earth – caused a fluke spin-off that drove evolution all the way to us today.

The next big extinction or scrape we managed to get through happened between 450–550 million years ago. This was a bit of a tricky situation, and the scientists named it dead simply to make it easy for us to remember. They called it the Ordovician-Silurian extinction event … rolls off the tongue, eh?! In this one, almost as much as 70 per cent of all life on Earth died out due to dramatic temperature changes and equally extreme sea level rises and falls.

Next up came the Devonian extinction about 375–560 million years ago and again around 70 per cent of life died out. And this nightmare didn't happen overnight. No, it lasted for about 20 million years. Then came the daddy of all extinctions. The Permian-Triassic extinction killed pretty much all marine life – 96 per cent to be precise – and 70 per cent of land animals, including most insects.

The insects give us a clue to how bad this extinction was, because scientists think of insects as the planet's hardiest of creatures. They are seen as robust – possessing superhuman properties that make them almost indestructible and the ability to survive even a nuclear holocaust – yet this one nearly did them in.

After all that, you would think things would start to calm down a wee bit, but no! Next, up rocked the Triassic-Jurassic extinction 201 million years ago. This killed off 75 per cent of species but, importantly, this one is believed to have cleared the stage for dinosaurs to get a foot (or claw) in and so the great era of the dinosaur began.

Sadly, Mother Nature had it in for them too and by 66 million years ago they were gone as well in the Cretaceous-Paleogene extinction, when 75 per cent of life died out. The lucky ones were bird-like dinosaurs who survived, and the birdies you see today are their descendants. Here the culprit is thought to have been a huge asteroid hurtling through space before whacking into Earth and causing a giant crater just off the coast of the Yucatan peninsula in Mexico. The massive impact of this collision raised so much dust that it blocked out the sun and the old routine for food stopped. Basically, with no energy from the sun, the plants could no longer photosynthesise and make food. In other words, the lights went out.

Two further extinctions followed – the Ordivician and Late Devonian caused global cooling, which killed the plants once more, then the Permian did the opposite and made the planet too hot and, you guessed it, the plants took the hit again. The threat of this happening again is what we are most worried about now. Global warming could be the trigger for the next big event.

And that brings us up to now. Phew. With all these extinctions it's a wonder we even made it this far!

DEAD END EARTH

Other ways we could croak it include death by an asteroid or a giant gamma ray burst, which sounds cool, but trust me it won't be cool at all. This mega blast of energy would come from a distant star. Basically, the energy volume gets turned up to a massive extent and the blast would strip the Earth of its ozone layer. The ozone layer does lots of useful things for us, including protecting us from dangerous UV radiation. A zap from a distant star like this would wipe out 70 per cent of all life, and that includes us. We would literally be toast! Sounds depressing. But the chances of an asteroid attack or gamma ray blast are very, very small. They are random, once-in-a-blue-moon events, although you never know. Given what's happened in the past, the next big extinction event is likely to be a long way off.

The eventual warming and expanding of the sun, combined with the eventual drop in atmospheric carbon dioxide, could cause the biggest mass extinction event in Earth's history and would spell the

end of all life. As the sun expands (which will happen millions of years from now), it will boil away the oceans, increase the breakdown of rocks from weathering (which has the effect of lowering carbon dioxide) and kill plant life on Earth, since plants need carbon dioxide and water. With all photosynthetic life now gone, all aerobic life (which needs oxygen from the plants) will also die off. This will leave behind the ancestors of the first cells on Earth, which are anaerobic bacteria. These too, though, will eventually die out from the heat of the sun. Life on Earth will have been burnt away.

Life's journey will then be complete, starting with the first cell 4.2 billion years ago, going through all the trouble of evolving all those millions of species including us, only to end up back where it all started, with a single-celled anaerobic bacteria, which itself will die. Cheery, isn't it?

PREPARING FOR THE WORST

There is still the possibility that, instead of an asteroid wiping us out, or the sun eventually killing us, other more immediate things might kill us off. This is known as anthropogenic extinction, or extinction caused by humans. What might the risks be of that? Nuclear annihilation has always hung over us. A hypothetical World War III could kill us all off. Surely, we wouldn't be that stupid, though. Right? Right?! A more likely event (although still unlikely) is some kind of pandemic involving a virus, or maybe even an antibiotic-resistant bacteria. After all, COVID-19 has had a rather good go at it.

Aside from these possibilities, we enter a world that is more like the science fiction of comic books and movies. Some say we will be overthrown by super-intelligent entities (no, not a team of maths teachers), which will outsmart us and take us as slaves or simply annihilate us. Others think we could make a mini-black hole that will suck up the whole Earth – this was actually a fear when we started messing with physics experiments at the LHC. Luckily for us, it didn't happen. Yet.

All these doomsday fears have sparked strange reactions in certain parts of the world. In the USA, in particular, the idea of the end of the world is fuelling big business. You see, extreme events spark people's natural fear. The USA has had some serious weather events with everything from wildfires, hurricanes and droughts through to devastating floods and freezing temperatures. If it couldn't get worse, they have also faced some major earthquakes and live with the threat of a mega-volcanic eruption from Yellowstone. As the planet has happily been kicking the life out of the poor Americans, they have done what humans usually do in life-threatening circumstances and got scared ... real scared.

Many think the end is nigh and they are stocking up on everything from freeze-dried cans of food and gas masks through to full-on nuclear bunkers (or should that be bonkers). Laugh as we might, there is a full-on survival shopping list to be had. Head down to the local mall or go online and you can get:

- A CBRN suit for a snip at $500 – this snazzy name stands for: Chemical, Biological, Radiation and Nuclear attack, but don't wear it to school. It's definitely not in style this season.
- A hazmat suit at a bargain $129.95 – but beware! You will look like something from *The Walking Dead* and people will move away from you at bus stops.
- The classic gas mask for around $200 – ironically, they are hard to breath in properly and you will sound like you have really bad asthma or a cross between Darth Vader and a malfunctioning robot.
- Your own body armour for around $250 – most suppliers offer gift cards if you're stuck for Christmas gift ideas.

Any of these possible doomsday events, though, is very much in the future. Humans will in all likelihood have evolved into some other kind of species, which we may not even recognise. Predictions as to how we might evolve include less muscle mass (since machines will do all the heavy lifting), weaker eyes (since visual aids will be commonly used) and perhaps less body hair. And you thought evolution would turn you into some sort of superhuman of the future? The changes just mentioned have turned you into the hero known as 'Baldy-Specky-Wimpy-Human' … just as you imagined it.

Maybe our genes will carry on in some other species, as we saw with the Neanderthals, some of whose genes continue in us. Or our genes may end up in some strange human/computer hybrid, in the form of a cyborg, who may live on another planet. These cyborgs might come back to the smoking remains of Planet Earth, dig down into the rubble, and come across the tattered pages of a book. This book. If you're reading this from the future – hello! How's the food?

CHAPTER 19

THINGS
WILL
ONLY
GET
BETTER

ESPITE THE RISKS we clearly pose to ourselves and the predictions of the glass-half-empty gang, things are actually looking good for the good old *Homo sapiens*. Think about the little man in your town who has a placard, a loudspeaker and a helper to hand out endless leaflets to tell you 'You are doomed! You are going to die! You will fry endlessly somewhere soon! The world will end at midnight if you don't take action!'

Well, let's think about it. What action does one need to take in this instance? And if you know the lights go out at midnight, why are you standing here in the high street and not saving us – or at least yourself? And, by the way, weren't you here last Saturday saying the exact same thing?

In defence of the naysayers, there are still a lot of terrible things going on here on Planet Earth. There are wars, famine and crime. There is cruelty and inequality and hardship all over the world. But overall, today things are as good as they have ever been for the human race. Science, technology and agriculture have all combined to give us a pretty good gig.

Now, it must be admitted that there was a time when agriculture brought much misery and inequality. There were millions of workers who had to toil in the field for the boss. These people were, in fact, slaves. Back in the 1800s, only a tiny number of people had a high standard of living. So, what did the lucky few look like back then?

Well, you needed certain status symbols to stand out from the ordinary. Firstly, you had lots and lots of money. And a castle, as well as staff to clean the castle and feed you. Oh! And an army to protect the castle, in case dirty, poor, diseased people dared knock on your door and ask for a chicken wing. The cheek!

WINNING STREAK

Since then, though, things have been on the up and up. We have never lived longer and we have never been wealthier. Today, a whopping 90 per cent of people on Earth do not live in extreme poverty and there are so many more of us now with the global population increasing sevenfold in these past 200 years. We have increased productivity and we have better homes, better food, better clothes, better working conditions.

Another big development has been education. In the past, only a tiny proportion could read and write. Some 1,500 years ago that was restricted to the clergy, who learned to read because of the Bible, or to civil servants who served the king. They were mainly tax collectors who gathered in all the king's money. Reading must have been seen as an odd thing to do back then when there was work to be done and fields to farm. Reading and writing were for the wealthy. They could lounge around in Greece thinking deep, meaningful thoughts. To put it another way, in 1800 there were 120 million people who could read and write. Now there are 6.2 billion, and it looks like they're all on Instagram. But from the looks of what they're posting, they might need a reading refresher ...

By the 1930s, one in three of us could read and write to an acceptable level, and today 85 per cent of people on the planet are literate. This is why school is so, so important to how far a human can go. Education is the key to all progress. Without it, we don't have scientists, engineers, businesspeople or doctors. Being able to think, reflect, question and debate actually stops wars. As a result, teachers are invaluable (I know, don't tell them or they'll never wipe that smug look off their faces).

Health is also on the up! In 1800, 43 per cent of babies died before they could reach the age of five. To put it another way, if a mother had two babies, one of them was likely to die before reaching five. In 1915, the average life expectancy was 35. To live into your forties was to become a wise and very old man. Today, however, the average life expectancy in Ireland is 78.3 for a man and 82.7 for a woman. This amazing feat isn't just due to new medicines. Other things helped as well.

Poor sanitation was a big factor – too much poo, not enough clean water – that led to more infectious diseases, which led to more deaths. It happened because of the switch from us being nomads who travelled around a lot in small gangs to being settled farmers clumped together, leaving our rubbish all around us. Then we started to get better food, which boosted our immune systems, which made us stronger and much better at fighting infections. There was better housing, and sanitation moved from outside – yes, people pooed outside on the street – to indoors, where it could be safely flushed away.

Other key developments that have helped us include breakthroughs in the worlds of science and medicine. Science became a real profession (trust me, it did) because of a better education system. These big-brained scientists were then ready to make the biggest and best scientific breakthroughs we have ever seen. Maybe one of the best was the so-called 'germ theory of disease' offered by Robert Koch and some of his mates. At the time, the science world probably thought old Koch and his gang were nuts. After all, the idea that tiny, microscopic creatures were causing massive diseases like TB, which destroyed people's lungs, would have seemed ridiculous. But it was a very important finding and it meant that something as simple as a doctor washing their hands when moving from a post-mortem of a dead person to delivering a baby made a very big difference. People were shocked when they realised that a big reason for infant deaths was down to dirty doctors!

Germ theory then became the springboard for the discovery of antibiotics and vaccines. This then meant that public health agencies were established to monitor and treat the health of people. This was a big help when giving vaccines to people. As we know ourselves from our COVID experience, when everyone has been vaccinated, everyone wins because of so-called 'herd immunity'. This is where a certain percentage of the herd has to be vaccinated to outdo the germ. If you do that, then the germ literally has nowhere to go because it doesn't have enough hosts to hide in and so it goes bye-bye.

Vaccines have made a huge contribution to human health. One big culprit, polio, has almost been eliminated from the face of the Earth. Smallpox, which haunted the people of the Dark Ages, is now gone completely. Without a vaccination plan, about 4 million cases of measles occurred in the USA each year. After the measles vaccine was introduced in 1963, measles was almost eliminated too, with only 667 cases reported in 2014.

The next biggy was antibiotics. Without them even today, people would continue to die of infectious diseases, which would return as the commonest cause of death. Surgery could not be performed without these guys due to the risk of life-threatening infections in your wounds. That is the reason for another big worry, which is called 'antibiotic resistance'. If we ever get a situation where bacteria manage to evolve to be resistant, then the world will be a very different place to what it is today. That would be a major step back and the big breakthroughs we have just mentioned in this chapter will be seriously reduced, taking us back to a time pre-antibiotics. We need to hope that we can use all of our clever scientific tools to outwit the bugs. If we don't, they will kill us. Can you hear them? They're laughing at us now as we speak. But I know that one day, you, or someone like you, might well find the next big breakthrough.

The population on Earth has exploded due to decreases in infant and overall deaths with less poverty. Population growth happens because of high fertility and low mortality. And, strangely, a decrease in child deaths comes with a decrease in the birth rate. At first, this doesn't seem to add up, but it appears that once mothers realise that the chances of their baby dying have decreased, they in turn have fewer children. The overall result of these trends is that population growth comes to an end, which is increasingly the case here on Earth. There is even a model for it, and it shows that countries that industrialised first like the UK took about 95 years for fertility to decline from more than six children per woman to less than three. Other countries that have industrialised more recently had an even faster demographic transition. South Korea went from 6 babies per mother to fewer than 3 in just 18 years.

However, despite this slowdown in baby manufacturing, the global population has increased fourfold during the twentieth century and current projections are that the Earth's population will stop growing around 2075, and will then start to decline. One thing is clear about the booming baby business: for girls, education can change far-ranging things. The clever science researchers found out that as a girl's years of education go up, the number of babies she has goes down. Education appears to broaden horizons. More and more of the world's population are getting themselves educated, and the money spent on education is never wasted.

That leads us nicely to the final thing that has made us humans so clever – peace. The clever experts tell us that one of the key purposes of a university education is to make people reasonable. To be able to talk, to debate with one another and not take your football back and stamp off into the house when you're annoyed. The ability to not fight with people is critically important in stopping the big fights or wars. Back in the 1980s, military experts, the ones who study big scraps, noticed something amazing. War – what had been the single biggest cause of death on Earth other than infection – had mostly stopped. It has its own name too. It is called the 'long peace', and it has lasted for more than 40 years now. However, recent conflicts in the Middle East and Ukraine have threatened this long peace. People may be forgetting how to share their football ...

So, as a species, more of us are richer than ever before, and we're living longer, healthier lives. More of us are well-educated. And we're not being drawn into needless wars. So why is it that most people think things have got worse and will continue to do so, despite the evidence staring them in the face? Recent studies have shown that only 10 per cent of Swedes think things will get better. The number was 6 per cent in the USA and 4 per cent in Germany.

Psychologists call this phenomenon 'cognitive dissonance'. An example is where what you see (e.g. a death on TV) points to one thing, but the data doesn't agree (e.g. lots of people still being alive). Most people assess the world from Facebook or Twitter. As long as they see that violence hasn't vanished, that there are still explosions and wars going on, they will have a negative outlook. This is in spite of the fact that the vast majority of people aren't involved in these events. One problem is that no one wants to report on peace – it's boring and doesn't sell newspapers.

Perhaps this is a safety mechanism. We are drawn to the worst-case scenario to protect ourselves. To batten down the hatches against the storm that might come. The cave person who stayed in their cave was more likely to survive – even if the storm was only a shower. Only by gathering the data (a very important role for all scientists), analysing it and tracking it over time do we get an accurate picture. That's why it's so important for us to read past the shocking headlines into the real facts.

Remember the motto of the Royal Society in London: 'Take nobody's word for it'.

THE LAST STOP

So let's recap. Life for us began as a single cell. Evolution then played out according to Darwin's theory of evolution. Life then became a fight. Cells were in competition with each other for resources, which would allow for yet more evolution. Bacteria, plants, animals, dinosaurs, all to get to us: hairless apes that walk on two feet. It was a chance in a million or more for all this to happen. It all could have been so different. Our ancestors could have become extinct in one of the great extinction events. The dinosaurs could have survived to rule the roost, leaving little room for us. But we've made it this far, so let's keep going.

As a species, we're curious, so we began to discover all kinds of interesting things. But life was horrible for the vast majority of people for a very long time. Poverty, sickness, death, wars – all lumped on us for reasons that were never fully explained.

And then, things began to get better. Educated scientists and engineers came along to help. Engineers came up with sanitation strategies. Scientists discovered drugs to kill bacteria. Things then improved and improved, and the course of history went up, up, up. More people are living in peace, longer than ever before. We have worked out that killing each other was, well, killing us. In a nutshell, we are living longer and we are wealthier and healthier than at any time in our entire existence.

What will continue to improve? Will there be more and more people out of poverty? Will we prevent or cure diseases that still affect us? Will the world become more equal? Will robotics and artificial intelligence make a huge difference to our lives?

We control our environment like no other species before us. As long as we stop making a hames of it by threatening the water or food supply, or continue to destroy our environment, we should be fine.

Every single human being on Earth has a right to enjoy the benefits of all the science that's been done in their name and for future generations. It's been done out of curiosity. It's been done to make things better, either through enlightenment or for practical benefits. It's been done to enhance the lives of people.

But the world needs new people to make sure we continue this winning streak. It needs people who can think, and study, and wonder, and listen. People who will 'take nobody's word'. People who will boldly go where no one has gone before ... people like you.

Sure what else would you do with your precious time on this spinning lump of rock? Live long and prosper, my friends. It's a cool world you're going to make a difference in!

INDEX

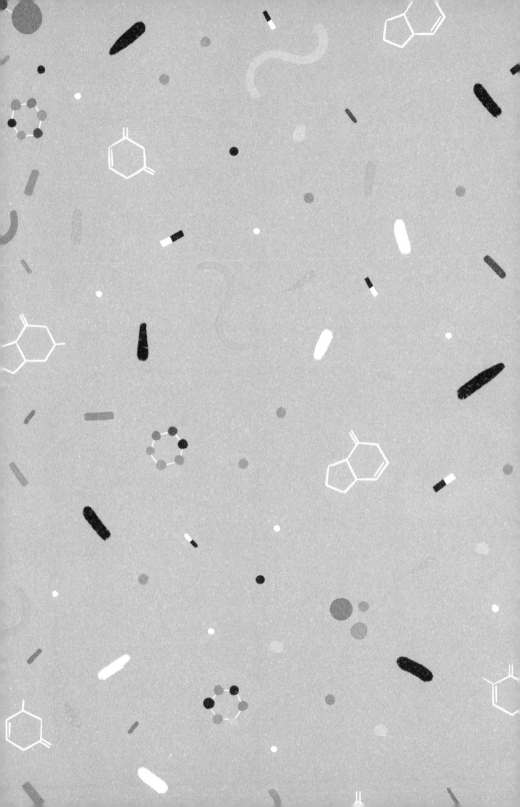